Collins

175 YEARS OF DICTIONARY PUBLISHING

Improve Your

Writing Skills

HarperCollins Publishers
Westerhill Road
Bishopbriggs
Glasgow
G64 2QT

First published 2000 as *Collins Wordpower
Good Writing*
Revised edition published 2004 as
Collins Good Writing Skills
This edition published 2009

Reprint 10 9 8 7 6 5 4 3 2 1 0

© 2000, 2004, 2009 Estate of Graham King

Cartoons by Hunt Emerson

ISBN 978-0-00-728805-2

A catalogue record for this book is
available from the British Library

Printed in Great Britain by
Clays Ltd, St Ives plc

Contents

GRAHAM KING (1930-1999)

Graham King was born in Adelaide on October 16, 1930. He trained as a cartographer and draughtsman before joining Rupert Murdoch's burgeoning media empire in the 1960s, where he became one of Murdoch's leading marketing figures during the hard-fought Australian newspaper circulation wars of that decade. Graham King moved to London in 1969, where his marketing strategy transformed the *Sun* newspaper into the United Kingdom's bestselling tabloid; subsequently, after 1986, he successfully promoted the reconstruction of *The Sunday Times* as a large multi-section newspaper.

A poet, watercolourist, landscape gardener and book collector, Graham King also wrote a biography of Zola, *Garden of Zola* (1978) and several thrillers such as *Killtest* (1978). Other works include the novel *The Pandora Valley* (1973), a semi-autobiographical account of the hardships endured by the Australian unemployed and their families set in the 1930s.

In the early 1990s, inspired by the unreadability and impracticality of many of the guides to English usage in bookshops, Graham King developed the concept of a series of reference guides called The One-Hour Wordpower series: accessible, friendly guides designed to guide the reader through the maze of English usage. He later expanded and revised the texts to create an innovative series of English usage guides that would break new ground in their accessibility and usefulness. The new range of reference books became the Collins Wordpower series, the first four titles being published in March 2000, the second four in May 2000. Graham King died in May 1999, shortly after completing the Collins Wordpower series.

Introduction

Having picked up this book the odds are that you are a writer. Perhaps not a journalist or a novelist, but a writer nevertheless: of letters, memos, reports or even an occasional note to the milkman. You may keep a daily diary, or limit your output to greetings on Christmas cards once a year.

There is also a good chance that you suddenly have a *need* to write – a job application perhaps, a ticking off to the council, a heartfelt letter of condolence to a friend. Mind and pen poised, it slowly dawns on you that the gap between what you want to say and what hesitantly appears on the paper in front of you is as wide as an ocean.

Can you learn how to improve your writing skills? Can the art of good writing be taught? Despite some opinions to the contrary, the answer is yes. Writing is a highly personal accomplishment and while some will spectacularly develop native talents others will always find it a frustrating slog. But *everyone* is capable of enhancing their powers of written communication simply by learning and practicing the basic principles of clear, concise and coherent writing: **planning**, **preparation** and **revision**. Further improvement comes from observing examples of good and also bad writing, and your confidence as a writer will grow as you begin to appreciate that the English language is not a fearsome book of rules but an unrivalled communications tool that you can learn to use with the familiar ease of a knife and fork.

It is important at the outset that you are aware of the difference between speech and writing. You may think, 'If only I could write as easily as I speak!' Unfortunately it's a wish that's rarely granted. When we talk to someone face to face (or even over the phone) we can instantly correct mistakes and clarify misunderstandings, provide subtle nuances with a smile, a laugh or a shrug, add emphasis with a frown or tone of voice. But when we write something, we have just one shot to hit the bullseye so that whoever reads it understands it – precisely. Two millennia ago the Roman orator Cicero offered a pretty good tip: the point of writing is not just to be understood, but to make it *impossible to be misunderstood*.

The ability to write well is a valuable, life-enriching asset and *Collins Good Writing Skills* will help you towards this goal. Much of what you will read is the lifetime word wisdom of a veteran national newspaper sub-editor. Sub-editors are a newspaper's front-line defence against inaccurate, ungrammatical, long-winded, repetitious and pompous writing – and thus the reader's best friends. A group of *Daily Telegraph* sub-editors decided that a new shorter 60-word police caution was still too ponderous and proceeded to distil the same meaning into 37 words. Here is the 60-word version, devised by a Scotland Yard committee :

> *You do not have to say anything. But if you do not now mention something which you later use in your defence, the court may decide that your failure to mention it now strengthens the case against you. A record will be made of anything you say and it may be given in evidence if you are brought to trial.*

And here is the revised, sub-edited version, clearer and shorter:

> *You need say nothing, but if you later use in your defence something withheld now, the court could hold this against you. A record of what you say might be used in evidence if you are tried.*

No long or obtuse words, no flowery phrases – just crystal-clear prose that makes few demands on a reader's time, holds the reader's interest throughout and simply can't be misunderstood. That is the kind of model this book recommends, although you will also be amused and appalled by dozens of other masterpieces of a vastly different kind – masterpieces of drivel and obscurity to drive home the sort of writing to avoid.

Into the jungle, with machete and pen

But first, let us be brave. We are about to hack our way through a jungle. The dense, tangled world of obscure and impenetrable language. Officialese. Circumlocution. Tautology. Gobbledegook. Jargon. Verbosity, pomposity and cliché. All the ugly growths that prevent us from understanding a piece of writing.

Perhaps the obstacle is a notice from our bank, the district council, the water, gas or electricity supply company, which for all we know might have a serious effect on our future. Or it may be a newspapaper or magazine article that makes us stop in mid-sentence to realise that we do not understand its meaning. Or perhaps it's an advertisement for a job we might fancy . . . if only we knew what the wording meant.

This book, however, is not intended to help the baffled reader to fight through the thickets of spiky legalisms, prickly abstractions and tangled verbosity. Rather it is a guide to help you, the **writer** of the letter, memo, report or CV, to make sure your writing is clear of such obstacles to understanding.

Don't be a sloppy copycat!

In business and bureaucracies, it is fatally easy to fall in with the writing habits of those around you: sloppy, vague and clumsy.

Yet most of us realise that a letter, memo or report from someone who knows how to write clearly and with precision is obviously more welcome, and read more keenly, than a dreary wodge of waffle and wittering.

Your own writing will be most effective when it is clear and direct. People who write in a straighforward way always shine out against the dim grey mass of Sloppies.

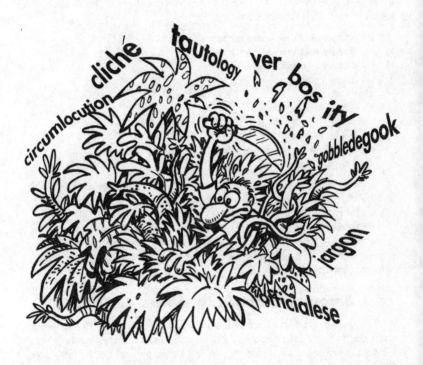

To be a good writer you have to write tighter

The usual advice on clear expression is: 'Write as you speak'. But we have already concluded that unless you have special gifts or professional skills, this is virtually impossible. Perhaps the advice should be amended to: 'Write as you speak – say what you mean, but make it tighter'.

One simple way to accomplish this is always to think economically. Less is often more. Some of the greatest thoughts and concepts in history have been expressed in surprisingly few words. The Ten Commandments are expressed in just 130 words; the Sermon on the Mount in 320, Kipling's poem 'If' is less than 300 words long and the American Declaration of Independence was made in 485 words.

On the other hand a recent EEC internal memo on aubergine production and marketing issued in Brussels hit a word count of 9,800! Of all these, which would you think is the most readable?

The same applies to words: shorter is better. Many famous writers of the past were experts at saying what they meant in very few words, and simple, often one-syllable words at that. Milton and Shakespeare were deft users of simple words but for beauty achieved through sheer simplicity it is hard to beat Robert Herrick's *The Daffodils*:

> *We have short time to stay, as you,*
> *We have as short a spring;*
> *As quick a growth to meet decay,*
> *As you, or any thing.*
> *We die,*
> *As your hours do, and dry*
> *Away,*
> *Like to the summer's rain;*
> *Or as the pearls of morning's dew*
> *Ne'er to be found again.*

With the exception of just a few words (*decay, away, summer's,* etc) every word of this stanza is of a single syllable, perhaps symbolic of the brevity of life, and it is a model that every writer could aspire to.

Of course economy of expression isn't everything and it can be misleading to argue the toss between long and short words, concrete or abstract nouns, active or passive voices. What is important is selecting the *right* word, and putting it in the *right* place for the *right* reason.

Before you begin to write . . . THINK!

Another English writer, William Cobbett, declared that 'He who writes badly thinks badly'. You could usefully reverse this. A minute's thought before a minute's writing is advice worth thinking about, perhaps on the following lines:

- What do I want to say?
- Am I making just one main point, or several?
- If several, what's the order of importance?

You may find it worthwhile to jot down your points before starting your letter, or report, or story. Once you've organised your material you can then concentrate on expressing it in writing, getting the right words in the right places.

When you've completed your writing – and this is the vital bit – read it through and decide, as critically as you dare, whether you've got it right. Try to put yourself in the shoes of the reader. Is the meaning clear? Is it expressed directly? Is it interesting to read? How would I feel after reading it? If the answers to any of the first three questions is 'no' or even 'well . . . ' you should try to face up to rewriting it. Nobody pretends that rewriting isn't an unwelcome task but the reward is worth it – the satisfaction of having improved upon your first effort. Of course, if you use a word processor the job of rewriting (often sentence by sentence or paragraph by paragraph) is easier.

Thinking before writing will help you avoid clangers like this paragraph from a bank's letter to a customer:

> *We will not charge the £19 and £23 fee if your account had an average*
> *cleared credit balance of at least £500 during the period we were charging*
> *for. If you only pay a charge as a result of a charge you paid in the*
> *previous charging period, we will refund this second charge if you ask.*

Pardon? Oddly enough, this piece of nonsense bore the Crystal Mark, the seal of clarity approved by the Plain English Campaign, which brings us to the two key organisations in Britain devoted to the elimination of drivel and gobbledegook and the encouragement of clear language and plain English.

The Golden Bull vs the Golden Rhubarb

The self-appointed guardian angel of our national tongue is Chrissie Maher, OBE, founder of the Plain English Campaign. Remarkably, Ms Maher, who was brought up by a widowed mother in a poor household in wartime Liverpool, did not learn to read or write until she was in her teens. The disability dogged her until, during a job interview with an insurance company, she admitted she was illiterate. Instead of rejection she was told she could have the job, provided she studied at night school; three years later she could read, write and count. In her adult life she went on to a degree course in sociology.

A deprived background made Chrissie Maher keenly aware of how uneducated people were fobbed off by officialese they couldn't understand, and how they were often coerced into signing important documents and forms, with little idea about what the small print meant. When she came across a case in which an old lady died of hypothermia because she couldn't understand the application form for a home heating grant, she decided to do something about it.

Maher launched the Plain English Campaign in 1979: since then, with its relentless exposure of bureaucratic pomp and absurdity, it has become both feared and admired. It prompted a government review which resulted in some 36,000 official forms being scrapped and another 60,000 rewritten to make them more easily understood. It is frequently hired by organisations to vet their forms and sales literature and issues a 'Crystal Mark' to commercial prose which passes its standards of clarity. To transgressors of simple English however, it issues its annual Golden Bull awards. Winners of this trophy – appropriately a pound of tripe – include the Department of Agriculture which defined cows, pigs and sheep as 'grain-consuming animal units', a car sales firm which described a used car as a 'pre-enjoyed vehicle', and the National Health Service for defining a bed as:

> *A device or arrangement that may be used to permit a patient to lie down when the need to do so is a consequence of the patient's condition rather than a need for active intervention such as examination, diagnostic intervention, manipulative treatment, obstetric delivery or transport.*

The more recent Plain Language Commission has identical objectives and issues its own annual awards – the Golden and Silver Rhubarb trophies for the year's most baffling documents.

Both organisations waged a war of blunt words in 1995 when the Commission awarded NatWest Bank a silver trophy for what it called an example of the year's worst gobbledegook in a booklet about mortgage rates, part of which read:

> *Depending upon the type of mortgage you have, repaying early can have certain financial consequences [sic], for instance, early repayment of a mortgage and surrender of an endowment policy, may leave you with a small surrendering sum, which may not reflect the actual monies invested. Alternatively, cancellation of a life policy without considering future needs may ultimately mean increased premiums for the same amount of life cover in the future.*

To the embarrassment of the Plain English Campaign, NatWest Bank had just been nominated for its 'Crystal Clear Bank of Europe' award for the 'ease with which its literature could be understood'!

You may wonder, when the experts in concise, coherent communication disagree so profoundly, whether you will ever see the clear light of day through the other side of the jungle. But take heart and read on and you will learn how even the most dense thicket of verbiage can be trimmed and tamed.

From Here To Obscurity

If language can be like a jungle sometimes, officialese is the minefield laid among the thorny thickets and clinging creepers. And despite the successes of the Plain English teams, officials in government, local councils and other bureaucratic organisations still too often try to lure us into their baffling word mazes.

The language of officialdom can obliterate all meaning. Feel the undergrowth closing in as you try to fight your way out of this trap dug by the former Department of Health and Social Services . . .

The Case of the Crippled Sentence

A person shall be treated as suffering from physical disablement such that he is either unable to walk or virtually unable to do so if he is not unable or virtually unable to walk with a prosthesis or an artificial aid which he habitually wears or uses or if he would not be unable or virtually unable to walk if he habitually wore or used a prosthesis or an artificial aid which is suitable in his case.

This would-be 'sentence' first of all reflects the legalistic terror of official punctuation: the full stop or comma which, if misplaced, might lead the Department all the way to a House of Lords appeal. And, second, it ignores or offends half the population – women – by exclusively using the masculine pronouns *he* and *his*.

So let us take our machete to the undergrowth, bring in the mine detectors and wire-cutters, and try to discover what, if anything, this passage struggles to convey. A step at a time, too, for fear of booby traps.

A person shall be treated as suffering from physical disablement . . . treated?

This is not intended as medical advice, but since the context is medical the reader may, however briefly, be confused. Lift out *treated* and replace with *considered*. Throw *treated* into the shrubbery.

Suffering from physical disablement. Why not simply *physically disabled*? And while we are at it, we don't need *as* after *considered*. Toss that into the shrubbery too.

So far, in our cleaned-up version, we have 'A person shall be considered physically disabled' – and we don't seem to have lost any of the intended meaning.

Such that he is either unable to walk or virtually unable to do so. Wrench away the clumsy *such that he is* and replace it with *which makes him* (we'll come to the offending pronouns later). Next, we cut out *either*, because we don't need it.

We now have *which makes him unable to walk, or virtually unable to do so.* This can be more tightly expressed as *which makes him, unable, or virtually unable, to walk.*

Peering into the darkening thicket we next tackle *if he is not unable or virtually unable to walk with a prosthesis or an artificial aid which he habitually wears or uses . . . **Stop!*** The rest is just the gibbering of jungle monkeys. This seems to mean that the person can get around, but only with the help of a prosthesis or other artificial aid. The word *even*, before *if he is not*, would have helped. But we really do not need this tangled heap of words at all.

The entire 'sentence', if it means anything, must surely mean this:

> *A person is regarded as physically disabled if he or she always needs an artificial aid to walk.*

We can of course replace the masculine and feminine pronouns with *that person*:

> *A person is regarded as physically disabled if that person always needs an artificial aid to walk.*

As you can see, the meaning remains clear. But what about the prosthesis, you may ask. Well, there are thousands of people with prostheses in the form of replacement hips and knees and other artificial body parts who are bounding about without the least need of any artificial aids – wheelchairs, zimmers and walking sticks – so the amended versions are perfectly valid.

The Case of the Crippled Sentence is a prime example of the need to think 'What do I want to say?' And then to say it, the simple way.

A serious case of effluxion

Here's a verbal smokescreen from a London borough council:

> *And take further notice that under the provisions of Section 47(2) of the said Housing Act 1974 in relation to any land consisting of or including Housing Accommodation in a Housing Action Area a landlord must not less than four weeks before the expiry by effluxion of time of any tenancy which expires without the service of any Notice to Quit, notify the council in writing that the tenancy is about to expire in accordance with the said Schedule 4 . . .*

This is a model of mixed officialese and legalese: you can almost see the glint of watch-and-chain on the Town Clerk's egg-stained black waistcoat. How do we turn it into something like English, without losing any legal force the passage might be required to have?

For a start, there appears to be no need for *And take further notice*. If the reader is not going to take notice, there seems little point in the writer's finishing this masterwork. Next: *under the provisions of Section 47(2) of the said Housing Act 1974* – the words *the provisions of* are redundant. Let's lose them. The same goes for *said*.

And next: *in relation to any land consisting of or including*. The lawyers can keep their *consisting of or including*, just in case they are struggling to cover, say, a backyard or front garden where someone lives in a caravan. But *in relation to* can be shortened to *concerning*. We have now brought *concerning* clumsily close to *consisting*, so let us replace *consisting of* with *that consists of*. The word *Accommodation* after *Housing* is not needed. And once *Housing* is left standing by itself, the capital *H* becomes even more obviously unnecessary.

Plodding on: *a landlord must not less than four weeks before the expiry by effluxion of time . . .* Quickly to the dictionary – to seek out the meaning of this excitingly unfamiliar word, *effluxion*. We find:

> **Efflux, n**. Flowing out (of liquid, air, gas; also fig.) That which flows out. Hence *effluxion*, **n.** See *effluence*, **n.**

From its meaning the word certainly suits the prose style, if nothing else. But we can do without *effluxion*. And we can also do without *expiry*.

Now, what is the rest of the message? It seems that in a Housing Action Area, if a landlord knows that a tenancy is running out and no notice to quit is needed, he must warn the council, in writing, at least four weeks before that tenancy is due to end. So let's tack that information on to our earlier repair:

> *Under Section 47(2) of the Housing Act 1974, concerning any land that consists of or includes housing in a Housing Action Area, if a landlord knows that a tenancy is due to end without need of a notice to quit, he or she must tell the council, in writing, at least four weeks before the tenancy runs out.*

The passage is no nail-biter and is still scarcely slick or smooth. But it *is* quite readable and clear and certainly less forbidding than the original mess.

How axiomatic is your bus shelter?

Here's a letter from the West Yorkshire Passenger Transport Executive:

> *I refer to your recent letter in which you submit a request for the provision of a bus passenger shelter in Ligett Lane at the inward stopping place for Service 31 adjacent to Gledhow Primary School. The stated requirement*

for a shelter at this location has been noted, but as you may be aware shelter erection at all locations within West Yorkshire has been constrained in recent times as a result of instructions issued by the West Yorkshire Metropolitan County Council in the light of the Government's cuts in public expenditure and, although it seems likely that the Capital Budget for shelter provision will be enhanced in the forthcoming Financial Year, it is axiomatic that residual requests in respect of prospective shelter sites identified as having priority, notably those named in earlier programmes of shelter erection will take precedence in any future shelter programme.

Let us briefly mop our brows and try to fathom what the poor, befuddled author intended to say, before we set about helping him say it in plain English.

At a guess, the passage could be summed up like this:

I refer to your request for a bus shelter in Ligett Lane . . . Unfortunately, because of Government spending cuts, West Yorkshire Metropolitan County Council has in turn ordered a curb on bus-shelter building. Although there may be more money for such work in our next financial year, shelters already on the waiting list will obviously be built first.

This seems simple enough, so where did the author go wrong? Let us lay his Frankenstein's monster on the dissecting slab:

I refer to your recent letter in which you submit a request for the provision of a bus passenger shelter in Ligett Lane . . . If the writer identifies the subject clearly enough, there is no need to remind his correspondent of all the details. The correspondent wants a straightforward Yes, No, or even Maybe – with an explanation, if the answer is No or Maybe.

The stated requirement for a shelter at this location has been noted . . . Of course it has. Otherwise the official would not be writing at all.

but as you may be aware . . . This is word-wasting. It doesn't matter if the correspondent is aware or not. The official's job is to make sure the correspondent knows the facts now.

shelter erection at all locations within West Yorkshire has been constrained in recent times . . . No purpose is served by *at all locations*. There is no reason to use *within* rather than *in*, no matter how widely this particular verbal fungus has spread.

constrained should be replaced by the easier-to-understand *restricted*; and *in recent times* is a redundancy. So is *as a result of instructions issued by*.

West Yorkshire Metropolitan County Council is rendered with a rare and forceful clarity, with not a syllable wasted. But then we slide back . . . *in the light of the Government's cuts in public expenditure . . .* The only meaning of *in the light of*, here, is *because of*. Your reader, rightly or not, will still blame the Government for the lack of a bus shelter, whether you use the clear or the foggy expression. So why head into the fog? (See *Fog Index*, page 75)

and, although it seems likely that the Capital Budget for shelter provision will be enhanced in the forthcoming Financial Year . . . The reader is less interested in what the bus shelter fund is called than what it will do for him, and when. So ditch *the Capital Budget*. And since a shelter is a shelter, *provision* is yet another unneeded word.

enhanced, in this context, means *increased*; there seems to be no reason to evade the more commonly-used word.

it is axiomatic that . . . Your dictionary will tell you that an *axiom* is a self-evident statement, a universally accepted principle established by experience; *axiomatic* here is presumably meant to convey *self-evidently true*. If something is that obvious, the official is wasting paper and his correspondent's time in saying it.

residual requests in respect of prospective shelter sites identified as having priority notably those named in earlier programmes of shelter erection . . . Thrusting the dissecting knife into the middle of this lot, we are left with *shelter requests not met by earlier building programmes* to which we add *will take precedence in any future shelter programme*. There's not a lot to argue about here, for once – apart, perhaps, from the repetition of *shelter programme*.

The deskbound, wordbound Frankenstein who created our monster may be saddened, even angry, at the way we have slimmed down his offspring. But at least he – and more importantly, his correspondent – can now discover what he really meant to say.

Missives such as our bus shelter letter don't have to be long to lose their way. Here's a paragraph from an insurance policy, hunted down by the Plain English Campaign:

> *The due observance and fulfillment of the terms so far as they relate to anything to be done or complied with by the Insured and the truth of the statements and answers in the Proposal shall be conditions precedent to any liability of the Company to make any payment under this Policy.*

Follow? Perhaps after five minute's concentration you might feel that you have fully understood it. The Campaign's recommended version would no doubt leave the insurance company gasping for words:

> *We will only make a payment under this policy if:*
>
> ● *you have kept to the terms of the policy; and*
> ● *the statements and answers in your Proposal are true.*

Almost all officialese can be analysed, dissected and rendered into clear and readily understood English but some is so dense as to resist the sharpest and most probing of scalpel blades. Here's an example, quoted by the *Daily Telegraph*, that consigns itself forever in the limbo of lost understanding:

> *ANY lump sum paid in accordance with Provision 7 of the Second Schedule shall be an amount equal to the Basic Nominal Fund that*

would be applied to calculate the Alternative Annuity under Provision 5 or Provision 12 of the Second Schedule on the assumption that the Annuitant had elected under Provision 4 of the Second Schedule that the date of his death was the Alternative Vesting Date or if greater an amount equal to the premiums received by the Society.

This is the sort of verbal hurdle that is still likely to confront average citizens at any time. Are we really expected to understand this guff? Or are we expected to hire a specialist or consultant to help us? Yet none of the sorry examples quoted here need have happened, if only the writers had held this conversation with themselves:

Q and A can save the day

Q   **What's it all about?**

A   It's about when somebody is classed as disabled/the special duty of a landlord in a Housing Action Area/someone wanting a bus shelter built.

Q   **What do we want to say?**

A   We want to say that someone who can't walk unaided is officially disabled; that a Housing Action Area landlord has to warn the council when there's about to be a tenancy available; that we can't afford the requested bus shelter just now.

Q   **Very well. So why don't we just SAY it!**

There is no excuse for obscurity. The English language, with its lexicon of nearly half a million words, is there to help any writer express any thought that comes into his or her head – even the virtually *inexpressible*. If we can't manage this, we should give up and leave it to others. Or admit our faults and learn how to do better.

The No-Good, the Bad and the Ugly: the Obstacles to Clear Communication

The long, long trail a-winding: Circumlocution

Bournemouth was on Monday night thrown into a state of most
unusual gloom and sorrow by the sad news that the Rev A M Bennett –
who for the last 34 years has had charge of St Peter's Church and parish,
and who has exercised so wonderful an influence in the district – had
breathed his last, and that the voice which only about a week previously
had been listened to by a huge congregation at St Peter's was now
hushed in the stillness of death . . .

Lymington Chronicle, January 22, 1880

When a writer or speaker fills you with the urge to shout 'Get on with
it!', he or she is probably committing the sin of **circumlocution** – roundabout
speech or writing, or using a lot of words when a few will do. In most of
today's newspapers the prose above would be a collector's item.

Politicians, of course, are notable circumlocutionists; perhaps it's an
instinct to confuse, to prevent them from being pinned down. A few years ago
a British political leader went on television to explain his attitude to the
introduction of a single currency for all countries in the European Community.

Before you continue reading, you should probably find a comfortable
seat . . .

No, I would not be signing up: I would have been making, and would
be making now, a very strong case for real economic convergence, not the
very limited version which the Conservatives are offering, so we
understand, of convergence mainly of inflation rates, important though
that is, but of convergence across a range of indicators – base rates,
deficits and, of course, unemployemt – together with a number of
indexes of what the real performance of economics are . . .

(Perhaps a brief tea-break would be in order here.)

. . . the reason I do that and the reason why that is an argument that
must be won before there is any significant achievement of union is not

14

only a British reason, although it is very important to us, it is a European Community reason: if we were to move towards an accomplished form of union over a very rapid timetable without this convergence taking place it would result in a two-speed Europe, even to a greater extent than now – fast and slow, rich and poor – and the fragmentation of the Community, which is the very opposite of what those people who most articulate the view in favour of integration and union really want; when I put that argument to my colleagues in, for instance, the Federation of Socialist Parties, many of whom form the governments in the EC, there is a real understanding and agreement with that point of view . . .

So what, precisely, might the gentleman have been hoping to convey? Probably this:

I do not want a single European currency until various other factors affecting the question have been dealt with. The factors are these . . .

A former US President, George Bush, was famous for his bemusing circumlocution, as in this speech defending his accomplishments:

I see no media mention of it, but we entered in – you asked what time it is and I'm telling you how to build a watch here – but we had Boris Yeltsin in here the other day, and I think of my times campaigning in Iowa, years ago, and how there was a – I single out Iowa, it's kind of an international state in a sense and has a great interest in all these things – and we had Yeltsin standing here in the Rose Garden, and we entered into a deal to eliminate the biggest and most threatening ballistic missiles . . . and it was almost, 'Ho-hum, what have you done for me recently?'

Circumlocution (also called **periphrasis**) typically employs long words, often incorrectly or inappropriately, and probably derives from a need to sound learned (a policeman referring to a bomb as an *explosive device*) or a desire not to offend (asking, for example, 'I wonder if you would mind awfully moving to one side' instead of the more direct 'Get out of my way!'. Some forms of circumlocution may be excusable, but most are due to unthinking use of jargon and clichés in place of more precise (and usually briefer) expressions. Typical is the use of *with the exception of* for *except; with reference to/regard to/respect to* for *about; for the very good reason that* for *because*, and so on.

To avoid being accused of circumlocution, **stick to the point!** If you intend to drive from London to Manchester in the most direct way possible you'd hardly wander off every motoway exit and then dither about along country lanes. The same principle applies to effective communication.

It also pays to be aware of persistent offenders – circumlocutory phrases many of us are inclined to utter when the exact, simple word we want fails to turn up. Here's a short list.

The Circumlocutionist's Lexicon

apart from the fact that – *but, except*
as a consequence of – *because of*
as yet – *yet*
at the time of writing – *now/at present*
at this moment/point in time – *now/at present*
avail ourselves of the privilege – *accept*

be of the opinion that – *think, believe*
because of the fact that – *because*
beg to differ – *disagree*
by means of – *by*
by virtue of the fact that – *because*

consequent upon – *because of*
consonant with – *agreeing/matching*
could hardly be less propitious – *is bad/unfortunate/unpromising*

due to the fact that – *because*
during such time as – *while*
during the course of – *during*

except for the fact that – *except/but*

few in number – *few*
for the reason that/for the very good reason that – *because*

give up on (it) – *give up*
go in to bat for – *defend/help/represent*

in accordance with – *under*
in addition to which – *besides*
in a majority of cases – *usually*
in all probability – *probably*
in anticipation of – *expecting*
inasmuch as – *since*
in association with – *with*
in close proximity to – *near*
in connection with – *about*
in consequence of – *because of*
in contradistinction to – *compared to/compared with*
in excess of – *over/more than*
in isolation – *alone*
in less than no time – *soon/quickly*
in many cases/instances – *often*
in more than one instance – *more than once*
in order to – *to*

in respect of – *about/concerning*
in spite of the fact that – *although/even though*
in the absence of – *without*
in the amount of – *for*
in the event that – *if*
in the light of the fact that – *because*
in the near future – *soon*
in the neighbourhood of/in the vicinity of – *near/about*
in the recent past – *recently*
in view of/in view of the fact that – *because*
irrespective of the fact that – *although*

large in size/stature – *large/big*

make a recommendation that – *recommend that*

nothing if not – *very*
notwithstanding the fact that – *even if*

of a delicate nature/character – *delicate*
of a high order – *high/great/considerable*
of the opinion that – *think/believe*
on account of the fact that – *because*
on a temporary basis – *temporary/temporarily*
on the grounds that – *because*
on the part of – *by*
owing to the fact that – *because*

pink/purple/puce, etc in colour – *pink/purple/puce, etc*
prior to – *before*
provide a contribution to – *contribute to/help*

regardless of the fact that – *although*

subsequent to – *after*

there can be little doubt that – *no doubt, clearly*
there is a possibility that – *possibly/perhaps*
to the best of my knowledge and belief – *as far as I know/I believe*

until such time as – *until*

with a view to – *to*
with reference to – *about*
with regard to – *about*
with respect to – *about/concerning*
with the exception of – *except*

17

People prone to pompous long-windedness can be gently reminded of their sins by quoting to them a well-known nursery rhyme rewritten in circumlocutory style:

> *Observe repeatedly the precipitate progress of a trio of sightless rodents: together they coursed apace on the heels of the agriculturalist's consort, who summarily disjoined their caudal appendages with a cutler's handiwork. One had never witnessed such mirth in one's existence as the incident involving those hemeralopic and nyctalopic mammals.*

The rhyme is, of course, *Three Blind Mice*.

An utterly unique added extra: Tautology

Mr and Mrs David Smith are proud to announce the birth of a baby girl, Sarah Anne.

Now, like 'Dog Bites Man', this isn't really news. But what if Mrs Smith had given birth to an *adult* girl? That *would* be news! Obviously Mrs Smith had given birth to a baby; it happens all the time. The newsy bit is that it was a girl.

The use of the word *baby* here is what is known as **pleonasm**, the use of redundant words. The same would apply if Mrs Smith invited the neighbours in to see her '*new* baby'. Are there any *old* babies? Of course all babies are new!

When a word repeats the meaning of another word in the same phrase it is called **tautology** and, usually, all verbal superfluities are known by this term.

Free gift! Added extra! Added bonus! These are exciting claims. And also wasted words: classic examples of tautology, the use of more than one word to convey the same thought.

A gift, if not free, is not a gift – except perhaps in the slang usage, 'That car was an absolute gift at £6,000'.

Something *extra* is clearly something *added*. And a *bonus* is normally an *addition*. Even if the word is used to describe something apart from money, an *added bonus* is an *added addition*. Nonsense, obviously. Yet we hear and read phrases such as *added bonus* every day, from people who have not thought what they are saying or writing, or do not care.

So accustomed are we to tautology in everyday speech and reading that this form of language misuse can pass unnoticed:

Will David's income be sufficient enough for you both?

How many of us would normally detect that *enough* is a wasted word?

Avoiding redundant words and expressions is a sign of a caring writer and here, to help you, is an A to Z of some of the more common superfluities.

An A to Z of Tautology

absolute certainty
actual facts (and its cousin, *true facts*)
added bonus/extra
adequate/sufficient enough
a downward plunge
advance warning
appear on the scene
arid desert
attach together
audible click

burn down, burnt up (*burn* and *burnt* by themselves are usually better)

circle round, around
collaborate together
connect together
consensus of opinion (it's simply *consensus*)
couple together
crisis situation

divide it up, divide off

each and every one
early beginnings
eat up
enclosed herewith, enclosed herein
end result

file away
final completion
final upshot
follow after
forward planning
free gift
funeral obsequies
future prospects

gather together
gale force winds
general consensus
grateful thanks

Have got (a common one, this. Simply *have* is fine)
the hoi polloi (as *hoi* means 'the', *the* is obviously redundant)
hoist up
hurry up

important essentials
in between
inside of
indirect allusion
I saw it with my own eyes (who else's?)

join together
joint cooperation
just recently

lend out
link together
lonely isolation

meet together
merge together
mix together, mix things together
more preferable
mutual cooperation

necessary requisite
new beginner, new beginning
new creation
new innovation, new invention

original source
other alternative
outside of
over with (for *ended, finished*)

pair of twins
past history
penetrate into
personal friend
polish up
proceed onward

raze to the ground (*raze* by itself means exactly that)
really excellent
recall back

reduce down
refer back
relic of the past
renew again
repeat again
revert back
rise up

safe haven
seldom ever
set a new world record
settle up
sink down
still continue
sufficient enough
swallow down

this day and age
totally complete
totally finished
tiny little child

unique means the only one of its kind. You can't get much more unique than that.
Not even *quite unique, absolutely unique* and *utterly unique*
unexpected surprise
unite together
unjustly persecuted
usual habit

very pregnant
viable alternative

warm 75 degrees (of course 75 degrees is *warm*!)
whether or not
widow woman

There are other forms of repetition, some intentional and some not. Writers have often used it for effect, for example in Samuel Taylor Coleridge's *The Rime of the Ancient Mariner*:

> *Alone, alone, all, all alone,*
> *Alone on a wide wide sea!*

Or in this equally famous passage from a speech of Winston Churchill's:

> *We shall go on to the end, we shall fight in France, we shall fight on the seas and oceans, we shall fight with growing confidence and growing strength in the air, we shall defend our island, whatever the cost may be, we shall fight on the beaches, we shall fight on the landing grounds, we shall fight in the fields and in the streets, we shall fight in the hills; we shall never surrender.*

Then there are those instances when, in writing, we manage to box ourselves into a corner with such irritating repetitions as, 'Her opinion *is*, *is* that it will never work'; 'The dealer admitted he *had had* the sideboard in his shop for two months'; 'Not *that that* would bother her in the least' and so on.

Finally, take care with **double negatives**, distant cousins of pleonasm. Although they can be useful they are also often confusing. *The bomb attack was* **not unexpected**. If you lived in a terrorist-ridden area, where to be bombed sooner or later would be no great surprise, the double negative *not unexpected* is better for conveying a suspended kind of expectation than *was expected* or *was no surprise*.

The puzzle for many writers is, why is *I **don't** know **nothing** about it* considered to be unacceptable, while *the Prime Minister is **not unmindful** of the damage already suffered* . . is grammatically respectable? The answer lies in the modifying power of the combination; *not uncommon*, for example, does not mean exactly the same as *common* but something between *common* and *uncommon* – 'a little more common than you might think'. The trouble is that often, double negatives can leave the readers trying to work out what is meant, so they are probably best avoided.

Witter + Waffle = Gobbledegook

*They never shorten anything – that would make it less important –
they inflate the language in a way they certainly oughtn't
to, indeed everything goes into officialese, a kind of gobbledygook
invented by the sort of people who never open a (hardcover) book.*

all things being equal
by and large
having said that
I am of the opinion
in the final analysis
last but not least
more than enough
the fact of the matter is
with all due respect

GOBBLEDEGOOK

That comment by poet Gavin Ewart refers to the propensity of ignorant people to witter and waffle and to inflate plain language into a meaningless, pretentious form of expression we recognise as **gobbledegook** (or gobbledygook).

'Witter words' are a key ingredient of gobbledook. Our language is liberally sprinkled with them – expressions that clog a sentence and add neither information nor meaning.

In this, wittering and witter words differ from circumlocution, which adds information, but in the wrong order – usually delaying the main point. In our death notice for the Rev A M Bennett (see page 14) the reader has to plod through 53 words before arriving at 'breathed his last'. But those 53 words did at least tell us the place and time of death, how long he had been a vicar, the name of the church, the extent of his influence and the reaction in his parish to the news.

Witter words, on the other hand, tell us nothing. Some are more often heard in speech (especially speeches by pundits and politicians) but many appear in writing.

For a classic example of wittering, loaded with witter words, we could hardly do better than this passage from a speech by former Australian Prime Minister Bob Hawke. Mr Hawke had so perfected his ability to say almost nothing in the maximum number of words that the style became known as 'Hawkespeak':

> *And that tends to mean at times if you want to put it, there is no point in running away from it, it tends to mean at times that there's a lack of specificity, or if you want to put it another way, there's a range of options which are put which are there to accommodate that indisputable fact about the social democratic parties such as ours.*

> *National Times*, November 22, 1985

Here's a compilation of witter words and phrases, many of which you'll recognise:

Witter Warning List

as it were
as such (as in *according to the rules, as such, they do not preclude* . . .)
absolutely (typically used instead of *yes*)
abundantly, abundantly clear
actually
all things being equal
as a matter of fact
as far as I am concerned
as of right now
at the end of the day

at this moment in time
a total of (as in *a total of forty-two applicants* instead of *forty-two applicants*)

basically
by definition
by and large (has anyone ever worked out the meaning of this?)

currently
curiously enough

during the period from (instead of *from January 16 to . . .*)

each and every
existing
extremely

funnily enough (usually precedes something that is not funny at all)

good and proper
good and ready

having said that (get ready for the contradiction!)

I am here to tell you
I am of the opinion that
I am the first to admit (how can you be so sure?)
I have to say, here and now
if you like
in a manner of speaking
in due course
in other words
in point of fact
in the final analysis
in view of the fact that
it goes without saying that (but I'll say it anyway)
I would like to say (and I certainly will)
I would like to take this opportunity to

last but not least
let me just say, right here and now
let us just be clear about this

may I make so bold as to say
many a time; many's the time that
more than enough; more than a little

never cease to wonder
(to) name but a few
needless to say

no two ways about it
not to mention

obviously
oddly enough
of course
of necessity (instead of *necessarily*)
on the basis of
once and for all
one and the same

precious few

quite
quite simply

really
rest assured

say nothing of (as in *to say nothing of last year's results . . .*)
shall I say (as in *it is, shall I say, a novel approach . . .*)
so much the better, so much the worse

the fact of the matter (as in *The fact of the matter is, the Government is wrong*, a form commonly used by politicians for *the claim I hope to get away with . . .*)
to all intents and purposes
to my mind, to one's own mind
to the point that

unless and until (as in *unless and until they pay, they can't board the ship*. Either word makes the necessary condition, so one of them is redundant.)

when all is said and done (not entirely meaningless but perhaps better replaced with *still/however/nevertheless*)
with all due respect, with the greatest respect
within the foreseeable future

y'know?

Here's a sentence which includes three witter phrases:

> **Needless to say**, we are, **if you like**, facing difficulties which, **when all is said and done**, we did not create ourselves.

The sheer lack of meaning in those phrases becomes more obvious when we find we can move them around the sentence, with no perceivable effect:

> We are, **if you like**, facing difficulties which, **needless to say**, **when all is said and done**, we did not create ourselves.

Or:

When all is said and done, we are, **if you like**, facing difficulties which, **needless to say**, we did not create ourselves.

Without the witter words the sentence is more forceful, half as long, and has not lost any of its meaning: *We are facing difficulties which we did not create ourselves*.

The second ingredient of gobbledegook is **waffle**; vague and wordy utterances that wander aimlessly along a path of meaning but effectively obscure it. In its extreme form it's called **verbal diarrhoea** or, more correctly, **logorrhoea**. When you combine this affliction with a good helping of witter words and a tendency to tangle your syntax the result is total obfuscation, or gobbledegook.

The former US President George Bush was an acknowledged master of gobbledegook – of using language (perhaps not intentionally, given his difficulties with English), not to reveal, but to obscure. Here he is, chatting with one of the astronauts on the space shuttle Atlantis: 'How was the actual deployment thing?' he asks. And again, this time in full flow when asked if he would look for ideas on improving education during a forthcoming trip abroad:

> Well, I'm going to kick that one right into the end zone of the Secretary of Education. But, yes, we have all – he travels a good deal, goes abroad. We have a lot of people in the department that does that. We're having an international – this is not as much education as dealing with the environment – a big international conference coming up. And we get it all the time, exchanges of ideas. But I think we've got – we set out there – and I want to give credit to your Governor McWherter and to your former governor, Lamar Alexander – we've gotten great ideas for a national goals programme from – in this country – from the governors who were responding to, maybe, the principal of your high school, for heaven's sake.

In 1944, a Texas congressman named Maury Maverick became so angry about the bloated bureaucratic language in memos he received that he described it as 'gobbledegook'. Explaining the name he said it reminded him 'of an old turkey gobbler back in Texas that was always gobbledy-gobbling and strutting around with ludicrous pomposity. And at the end of of this gobble-gobble-gobble was a sort of a gook'. Maverick was also the head of a federal agency, and promptly issued an order to all his subordinates: 'Be short and say what you are talking about. Let's stop *pointing up* programs, *finalizing* contracts that *stem from* district, regional or Washington *levels*. No more *patterns, effectuating, dynamics*. Anyone using the words *activation* or *implementation* will be shot'.

Half a century later it seems that the Maverick Edict has had little
he art world certainly never heard of it:

The spontaneous improvisation of trivial and fictional roles means a frame for social and communicative creativity which, by going beyond mere art production, understands itself as an emancipated contribution towards the development of newer and more time-appropriate behavior forms and a growth of consciousness . . .

Studio International, 1976

In a fit of liberalism you may excuse such babblings because writing about art is often incomprehensible anyway. But it is harder to excuse organisations supposedly dedicated to the art of human *communication*. Here is an extract from the Stanford University Press catalogue (1994) touting a forthcoming title called *Materialities of Communication*, edited by Hans Ulrich Gumbrecht and K Ludwig Pfeiffer:

Converging with a leitmotiv in early deconstruction, with Foucauldian discourse analysis, and with certain tendencies in cultural studies, such investigations on the constitution of meaning include – under the concept 'materialities of communication' – any phenomena that contribute to the emergence of meaning without themselves belonging to this sphere: the human body and various media technologies, but also other situations and patterns of thinking that resist or obstruct meaning-constitution.

Of course, to the normal person the first few words of a passage like this flash warning signs of impenetrability; to proceed would be to enter a mental maze from which there is no escape. But not all gobbledegook is that obliging. Much of it can entice you all the way through a wide and welcoming thoroughfare until, at the very end, you realise you are in a blind alley.

All the examples quoted in this chapter are real although it may seem at times that some genius made them up. Let them be a warning! Next time you are tempted to lapse into what reads or sounds like gobbledegook, remember that Texas turkey.

Smart talk, but tiresome: Jargon

The increase in £M3 was approximately equal to bank lending **plus** *the PSBR* **minus** *net sales of gilt-edged securities other than sales to the banks themselves.*

Nigel Lawson, *The View from No.11*, 1992

. . . the cognitive-affective state characterized by intrusive and obsessive fantasizing concerning reciprocity of amorant feelings by the object of the amorance.

US sociologist's definition of love, 1977

Most people recognise jargon when they see it: words and phrases that may have begun life within a particular circle of people, trade or profession, but which spread among others who merely wish to appear smart or up-to-date.

The *Collins English Dictionary* defines jargon as 'language characterized by pretentious synatax, vocabulary or meaning; gibberish'.

But not all jargon is pretentious or gibberish. It includes the shop talk of technical terms, understood by those who need to know and who have no need to explain it to outsiders. It is for millions of people a form of time-saving professional shorthand. It is a specialist's language designed for accurate and efficient communication between members of a particular group.

Fair enough. But too often, jargon and arcane verbiage are used by people to trick others into believing they know more than they actually do; or exploited as a security blanket to give them the feeling of belonging to an elite. This use – or misuse – can only interfere with meaning and understanding.

Hundreds of former valid scientific, technical. legal and technical terms have become more widely used as vogue or buzz words, and many of them are not properly understood. How many of us can hold hand to heart and say that we know precisely what these vogue words mean: *parameter, symbiosis, quantum leap, synergy, dichotomy, post-modern*? Yet despite our doubts we're still tempted to use them.

In spite of the efforts of the Plain English Campaign, jargon is still very much alive and kicking when we read of:

a visitor uplift facility	=	a tourist mountain train
ambient non-combatant personnel	=	war refugees
enthusiasm guidance motivators	=	cheer leaders
an unpremised business person	=	a street trader
festive embellishments (illuminary)	=	Christmas lights *
an ambient replenishment assistant	=	supermarket shelf stacker
wilderness recreation	=	camping and hiking
frame-supported tension structures	=	tents
unselected rollback to idle	=	aircraft engine failure in mid-flight

* True. This is how the politically correct Northampton Council described them.

The Job Ads Jargon Jungle

It is something of a paradox that where plain language is needed most, jargon is often used instead. This is perhaps best illustrated in job recruitment, where companies offering jobs have created their own hideous non-language:

> *Moving from hierarchical structures to a process-based architecture, our success has been based on consistent, integrated teamwork and quality enhancement through people. By ensuring consistency in the development and integration of process plans, you will facilitate the management processes to develop implementation plans for the processes they manage. You will also be involved in business plan modelling, rolling plan methodologies and the measurement of process effectiveness. As Integration Planner, your position will be at the interface of the personal, planning, implementation and measurement matrix.*

This example, quoted by the Plain English Campaign, prompts one to ask: 'Did anyone get the job, and if so, what are they doing?'

Here are some more cautionary examples of jargon from the same swampy jungle:

cultivational – fortunately a rare sighting, in an English National Opera advertisement for a 'Development Officer – Events', to be responsible for *co-ordinating and administering cultivational and fundraising events*. It is just possible that *cultivational* really means something. Our guess is that it is something to do with sucking up to people to get them to put money into a project. Your guess will be just as good.

driven – as in *quality-driven service organisation*. As with *orientated* (see under separate entry), this is merely meant to indicate the firm's sense of priority – in this case to offer high-quality services.

environment – meaning, usually, the place where the worker will do the job.
The firm that boasted of a *quality-driven* organisation also promised . . . *a
demanding and results orientated environment*. Another company required the
applicant to have a background of *progressive sales or marketing environment*.
In this case *environment* presumably meant *experience* or *business* – in which case
sales or *marketing* would have sufficed. *Progressive* can only mean 'forward-
looking' – and few firms would be looking for backward-looking candidates!
Yet another employer advertised for a worker who *should have experience in a fast-
moving, multi-assembly environment*.

Assuming that *multi-assembly* has its own meaning in the business
concerned, why not simply require *experience in fast multi-assembly*?

human resources – This term has now supplanted *personnel* which in turn
replaced *employees* or *workers*. *Personnel*, though also bureauspeak, at least does
not have the ghastly pretentiousness and pseudo-caringness of *human resources*.

motivated – one of the most hard-worked jargon words in job advertisements
. . . *the ability to motivate, lead and be an effective team player; management and
motivation of the sales force; should be self-motivated*. In the first two examples,
we can substitute *inspire* and *inspiration*. In the third, it is harder to guess
what the applicant will be required to prove. *Enterprising*, perhaps. Or *to show
initiative*. Or, if these sound too revolutionary for the company's taste, *able to
work unsupervised*.

orientated – as in *results-orientated environment or profits-orientated system*, is a
high-profile jargon word (as is *high-profile*). The word is presumably meant to
convey what a firm considers to be important. In these examples its use is
nonsense-orientated. A company that is not keen on getting results or profits will
not be placing job advertisements for much longer, so the phrase is redundant.
Another jargon version is *success-orientated* for the far simpler *ambitious*. And in
any case *orientated* is wrongly used for the shorter, original *oriented*.

pivotal role – Fancier version of *key role*. Neither helps much to explain a job.
If the importance of the position needs to be stressed, what's wrong with
important?

positive discrimination – In Politically-Correct speak this means providing
special opportunities in training and employment for disadvantaged groups
and ethnic minorities. However the term is still widely misunderstood and
perhaps best avoided. *Favoured* or *give preference to* might be better.

proactive – mostly found in social services advertisements describing the
approach to a particular job. It means initiating change where and when
needed as opposed to merely responding to events: *reactive*. Although a jargon
word, it is difficult to resist as there is no crisp single-word equivalent.

remit – meaning responsibility: *an experience-based understanding of multi-level personnel relationships will be within your remit.* Although *remit* may be shorter it is not otherwise commonly used, and is pompous.

remuneration package – simply means *salary and other benefits.*

skills – At first sight this is a reasonable word to expect in job advertisements. But there are some abuses, as in *interpersonal skills*, which presumably means *good at dealing with people.*

specific – as in *the key duties of the post will include developing country-specific and/or product-specific marketing activity plans.* Amazingly, that passage is from an advertisement placed by the personnel department of the University of Cambridge Local Examinations Syndicate. They could have said: . . . *developing plans for selling our products to particular countries.* But perhaps that sounded too boring.

structured – as in *it is likely that you will have worked successfully in a sizeable, structured organisation.* You would hardly go seeking recruits in an *un*-structured organisation, would you?

Not so long ago, schools had teachers, councils had social workers and everyone seemed to understand what they did. Now it is not so simple, and advertisements for jobs in education and social welfare contain more verbocrap than in any other field of human endeavour. Here's some impenetrable prose about a home for teenagers:

> *The aim of the home is to enable older young people who still have substantial emotional and personal deficits to make planned progress towards personal autonomy.*

Even among social workers this is garbled nonsense. Surely no professional catastrophe will happen if we simply say: *to enable teenagers with troubled personalities to learn to cope for themselves* . . . However, lacking in fashionable jargon, the rewrite would probably result in the original writer having a *job security deficit.*

The following example, from a publication of the former Inner London Education Authority, characterises the worst kind of jargon abuse:

> *Due to increased verbalization the educationist desires earnestly to see school populations achieve cognitive clarity, auracy, literacy and numeracy both within and without the learning situation. However the classroom situation (and the locus of evaluation is the classroom) is fraught with so many innovative concepts (e.g. the problem of locked confrontation between pupil and teacher) that the teaching situation is, in the main, inhibitive to any meaningful articulacy. It must now be fully realized that the secondary educational scene has embraced the concept that literacy has to be imparted and acquired via humanoid-to-humanoid dialogue. This is a break-through.* [and a load of jargon!]

Multicultural muddle

> *... experience of managing a multicultural urban environment and the ability to integrate equalities considerations into areas of work activity*

This passage, from an advertisement for a Deputy Director of Social Services, is a real polysyllabic mess. *Multicultural urban environment*, despite modern delicacies, simply means *racially-mixed part of town. Integrate* here may mean *build in*, or it may have been misused to mean *include*.

Every trade and profession is entitled to its own jargon – up to a point. So let us allow that *equalities* is readily understood among social services people as meaning equal treatment regardless of race, sex and, probably, physical handicaps – although the singular *equality* serves the purpose as well, or better.

That passage, converted into plain English, could read:

> *... experience of dealing with a racially-mixed town area and ability to ensure that equality is part of departmental life.*

The same advertisement also required *ability to organise intervention in the community to establish the needs of potential service users.* Meaning, presumably, *ability to go out to discover what people need us to do.*

Social workers do not have the field to themselves, when it comes to jargon. An advertisement for a health worker in Brazil announced:

> *You will assist the team in formulating and implementing a health policy, evaluating and developing appropriate responses to specific health problems in indigenous areas ...*

Meaning? Let's try to translate: *You will help to plan and carry out a policy to deal with health problems among local people.* Such a simplification may create a problem, however; to jargon-hardened health workers the revised job description sounds as though it's less important and so worth only half the salary of the inflated version.

Computerspeak and Psychobabble

As computing has evolved from cult to mass culture we can no longer ignore the jargon that computers have generated. Even quite young children are now familiar with dozens of terms: *floppy, prompt, menu, boot, megahertz, toolbar, drag* and *drop* hold no terrors for them. However some of the worst offences against the English language pour in an unending stream from the computer world:

> *Driven and focused by seeing the world from the customer's perspective, we continue to build an organisation where quality is embedded in every aspect of endeavour ... our continued growth in the network computing industry mandates that we now identify and attract the most talented and creative sales and marketing professionals ...*

Mandates? This announcement sounds as if it were written by someone whose dictionary had a bad coffee stain on the relevant entry.

Is writing jargon and management-speak more difficult than writing plain English? Many examples suggest that it is, yet its devotees persist in working harder than they need to. Whoever wrote this job description in an advertisement for a BBC position deserved his Golden Bull award: *The BBC seeks a Human Resources Assessment Technologist, Corporate Management Development*. But jargonising also offers a lazy way out. Here's a press release about a forthcoming conference, put out by the Association for Humanistic Psychology in Britain, which deserves full marks for sloth:

> *Conjoint Family Therapy, demonstration/participation workshop.*
> *This is a demonstration/participation workshop illustrating 20 to 30*
> *'ways of being' as therapist (i.e. 'self as instrument'/strategies/*
> *techniques) presented from an experiential-Gestalt/communications*
> *skills/learning theory/whatever else philosophical viewpoint. Emphasis*
> *is on experiencing . . . family/therapist/participant/self, the several*
> *modalities, strategies, values, processes, procedures, goals, dangers, fears,*
> *avoidance, growth and excitement of conjoint interaction.*

The author of that psychobabble should be made to stand in a corner and study an advertisement written in 100% plain English:

> *KITCHEN DESIGNER (Trainee considered) for thriving Chelsea studio.*
> *Drawing experience essential. Salary negotiable dependent on experience.*
> *If you are aged 20-30, educated to at least A-level standard, have a*
> *bright personality, thrive on hard work and are happy to work*
> *Saturdays, tell me about yourself by leaving a message on my*
> *Ansaphone, not forgetting to leave your name and phone no, or write*
> *a brief CV to . . . .*

Bright. Un-pompous. Direct. And, above all, *clear!*

The Jargonaut's Lexicon

Here's a list of jargon words and phrases that comply with the former US president Harry S Truman decree: 'If you can't convince 'em, confuse 'em'. The entries are graded with [J] symbols; the more elusive and impenetrable the jargon, the more [JJJs] it earns. Learn to recognise jargon, and avoid it if you can.

accentuate [j] *stress*
accessible [j] As in *We intend making Shakespeare accessible to the millions.*
Use *understandable, attractive*
accommodation [j] Use *home, where you live*
accomplish [j] As in *accomplish the task.* Use *complete, finish, do*
accordingly [j] Use *so*

accountability [j] Use *responsibility*

acquiesce [j] Use *agree*

acquire [j] Use *get, buy, win*

activist [j] As in *Liberal Party activist.* Use *worker, campaigner*

address [j] As in *we must address the problem.* Use *face, tackle, deal with*

adequate [j] Use *enough*

axiomatic [j] Use *obvious*

belated [j] Use *late*

blueprint [jj] As in *the proposal is a blueprint for disaster.* Use *this will end in, means/could mean disaster*

chair/chairperson [jj] Use *chairman, chairwoman*

challenged [jjj] As in *physically challenged.* One of a growing range of euphemisms for personal problems and disabilities. Even in these politically-correct times it is more acceptable to be frank but sensitive. Also avoid *differently abled.*

come on stream [jj] As in *the new model will come on stream in April.* Oil producer's jargon usually misapplied. Use *begin production, start working, get under way.*

come to terms with [j] Use *accept, understand*

concept [j] Use *idea, plan, proposal, notion*

core [jjj] As in *core curriculum, core concepts.* Use *basic*

creative accounting [jj] Not necessarily illegal but a vague and troubling term best avoided or left to the financial professionals.

cutback [j] A needless expansion of *cut*

de-manning [jjj] Use *cutting jobs*

de-stocking [jj] Use *running down stocks, shrinking*

downsizing [jjj] Usually meant to mean cutting jobs, or reacting to a bad financial year by cutting back production or services.

downplay [jj] As in *he tried to downplay the gravity of the case.* Use play down, *minimise.*

end of the day [j] As in *at the end of the day, what have we got?* Use *in the end*

final analysis [j] As in *in the final analysis it makes little difference.* Use *in the end*

front-runner [j] Use *leading contender, leading or favoured candidate*

funded [j] Use *paid for*

geared [jj] As in *the service was geared to the stockbroker belt.* Use *aimed at, intended for, connected to, suited to*

generate [j] Use *make, produce*

hands-on [jj] As in *he adopted a hands-on policy with the staff.* It makes you wonder what he was paid to do – massage them? Has been replaced by another jargon word, anyway – *proactive.*

heading up [jj] As in *Smith will be heading up the takeover team.* Use *heading* or *leading*

hidden agenda [jjj] Top-rank jargon. Use *hidden/disguised purpose*

identify with [jj] As in *He was identified with the activists*. Use *associated with, linked with*.

implement [jj] Use *carry out, fulfil*.

inaugurate [jj] As in *She will inaugurate the new policy*. Use *introduce, start*.

in-flight/in-house [j] Part of the language now but still jargon. When carried further, as in *in-car entertainment*, it can sound faintly ridiculous.

input [jjjj] As in 'A core post is available for a Senior Research Associate to take a leading role in the programme. The first projects involve relating nursing *inputs* to patient outcomes in acute hospitals' (University of Newcastle upon Tyne ad). A verbal germ picked up from the computer world where it is used as a verb meaning *enter* or *insert*, as in *he inputted the entire file*. Outside computing the word can mean *contribute* or, as a noun, *contribution*, or . . . nothing at all. Avoid.

interface [jjjj] Another refugee from computing. As a noun, it means *contact*. As a hideous verb, *interface with* can mean *work with, negotiate with, cooperate with* or simply *meet*. Any of these is preferable.

jury is still out [jj] As in *Whether the move has saved the pound, the jury is still out*. Use *is not yet known/decided/certain/clear*

meet with, meet up with [jj] Use *meet*

methodology [j] Often used in error for *method*. It really means *a system of methods and principles*

name of the game [jj] As in *the name of the game is to make money*. Use *object*

new high, new low [j] Use *new/record high level; new/record low level*

non-stopping [jjj] As in *the eastbound service will be non-stopping at the following stations* . . . Use *will not stop*

operational [j] As in *the service is now operational*. Use *now running/now working*

outgoing [j] Use *friendly*

overview [j] Use *broad view*

on the back of [jj] As in *the shares rose sharply on the back of the board's profit forecast*. Use *after/because of/as the result of*.

ongoing [jjj] As in *We have an ongoing supply problem*. Use *continuing/continual/persistent/constant*.

precondition [jjj] A condition is something that has to happen before something else will happen. A *pre-condition* is therefore nonsense, unless you wish to impose a condition on a condition! *There must be no preconditions for the peace talks* is questionable usage. Best to avoid and use *condition*.

put on the back burner [jj] Colourful, but jargon nevertheless. Use the more precise *postponed/delayed/deferred/suspended*, etc.

scenario [jj] As in *worst case scenario*. Originally meaning an outline of a play or film, its usage has been extended to mean *outcome* or *prediction*. Use the more specific words, or *result/plan/outline*, depending on context.

spend [jj] As in *their total advertising spend will exceed £7m*. A sloppy shortening of *expenditure* or *spending*.

state of the art [jj] Use *latest/newest*.

take on board [jj] Use *understand/comprehend/accept*

terminal [j] Use *fatal/mortal*

track record [j] Except for an athlete, perhaps, *track record* means nothing more than *record*. The next time you are tempted to use *proven track record*, be a brave pioneer and write *experience*

user-friendly [jj] Use *easy to use*

venue [j] Use *place/setting*

viable alternative [jj] Use *alternative/choice/option*

whitewash [j] As in *They'll certainly want to whitewash the incident.* Use *hide, gloss over, cover up, suppress, conceal*

Saying it Nicely: Euphemism

My father did not like the word fart. The first time I heard the word was when I was about three. I was watching a cowman milking and the cow farted. I said 'What was that?' and he said 'That was a fart'. It was just a word; as if I'd said 'what's that on the tree?' and he'd said 'bark'. I had a dog called Tuppy, because I bought him for tuppence. One day as I walked by him, I heard this same noise and I said 'Tuppy farted'. My father said, 'Where did you hear that?' and I said 'It came from his bottom'. However my father had a way of getting around the word. He would say, 'Who whispered?' and we totally accepted this euphemism until one day my granny says, 'Come, David, and whisper in granny's ear'.

Dave Allen, 1990 interview.

That's the trouble with euphemisms – they tend to be self-defeating because they paint a thick veneer over clarity and understanding.

Euphemisms – words and phrases people use to avoid making a statement that is direct, clear and honest – are often used out of kindness when the direct expression might give needless offence. For example a deaf person is often described as *hard of hearing* and a part-blind person as *partially-sighted*. Unfortunately, in recent times these traditional and harmless euphemisms have been extended and replaced with such terms as *aurally-* or *visually-challenged*.

Have you ever admitted that you might have been, well, to put it bluntly – drunk? How often have you heard someone honestly admit they were drunk? No, they might admit to having been *one over the eight, high spirited, squiffy, happy, a bit merry, worse for wear, tired and emotional* or any one of several hundred other euphemisms for drunkenness, but *drunk* – never!

Any user of the English language has to become something of an expert in understanding the true meaning of euphemisms, so much are they a part of our everyday lives. We need these seemingly innocent terms as replacements for those that are embarrassing, unpleasant, crude or offensive. We begin in the nursery with coy substitutions for organs and functions (*willy, winkle, thingy, botty, potty, tinkle, whoopsie, poo-poo, wee-wee, pee-pee*) and, from there, naturally graduate to adult equivalents: *John Thomas, old feller, down below, the 'loo* (or worse, *the bathroom*), *naughty bits, sleep with someone, nookie, jollies, hanky panky, rumpy-pumpy* and so on.

Our euphemistic skills are honed by the media which, though much franker nowadays, still maintain some taboo areas: *intimacy occurred* (had sex); *she was strangled and mutilated but had not been interfered with* (killed but not raped); *abused* (today's vague catch-all euphemism for any form of questionable physical, psychological or sexual activity). It is, as you can see, a very short journey from *sex-change operation* to *gender reassignment*.

The language of prudery also surprisingly invades that sanctum of directness, the doctor's surgery. Physician-speak is a growth area. *How're the waterworks? The ticker/tummy? Your stool? The back passage? The little lump?* All this prepares the way for *negative patient care outcome* to describe someone who dies in hospital.

The poor, in our euphemistic world, are *in a lower income bracket, under-privileged* or *fiscal under-achievers*. Slum homes are *inner-city housing*. When a city decides to clear away the slums the process is called *urban renewal* rather than slum clearance. And of course the same city calls its rat catchers *rodent operatives*.

Death has no dearth of euphemisms. Shakespeare might well ask today, 'Death, where is thy sting?' *Senior Citizens* and *Golden Agers* no longer simply die, they *pass on, pass away, depart, sleep with the angels, go to their just reward, go to a better place, take a last bow, answer the final call, pop off, go on a final journey, fade away or*, more jocularly, *kick the bucket*.

Euphemism is particularly effective for disguising crime – especially the crimes we might commit ourselves. *Tax fiddling, meter feeding, fare dodging, joy riding and being economical with the truth* all sound like commendable streetwise skills, whereas in fact they all amount to cheating and criminal activity.

Euphemism is also useful to help to make tedious-sounding jobs seem grand. Those people we used to know as insurance salesmen are now variously *financial advisers, investment consultants, fiscal analysts, savings strategists, liquidity planners, pensions counsellors* and *endowments executives*.

Again, the euphemistic traps are laid early in the career paths of young people. Consider these job descriptions and what, in real working life, they probably mean:

Pleasant working manner essential	Must be subservient
All the advantages of a large company	Nobody knows anyone else's name
Perfect opportunity for school leavers	Pathetically low pay
Salary negotiable	But only downwards
Earn money at home	Be exploited under your own roof
Earn £££££s!	But only through commission
Must have a sense of humour	Must not be a complainer

Euphemism and Political Correctness

The fertile breeding ground for euphemism today undoubtedly lies in the quest for what is popularly known as political correctness, or PC. The self-appointed guardians of political correctness quite commendably seek to banish stigmatising and dehumanising terminology from our speech and writing. They have been successful in removing from our everyday language such thoughtless and hurtful terms as *nigger, coon, cripple* and *OAP*; and no thinking person would now use the term *mongoloid* to describe a child suffering from Down's Syndrome. And they have been especially successful righting the centuries-old imbalance between the sexes in the popular perception: the use of *man* as a suffix or prefix (*manhandle, mankind, man-made, manpower, man in the street; foreman, chairman, one-man show, alderman, salesman,* etc); sexist generalisations (*doctors* are usually thought of as 'he', nurses as 'she'; *home helps* are always female, etc); and making writers, editors and broadcasters aware of the problem with the dominant male pronoun.

While much of this is desirable rethinking, and even necessary, the PC police have unfortunately taken a few steps too far and are consequently ridiculed by many reasonable people. The campaign to expunge the *E* from *VE Day* (Victory over Europe Day), in order not to offend our near neighbours during the 50th anniversary of the end of World War Two celebrations, succeeded only in offending millions of British families who had lost loved ones in the conflict.

The international campaign for so-called non-sexist language has led to what many people regard as euphemistic excess. Consider these recommendations from a recently-published manual from The Women's Press:

a grandfather clock	*should be called*	*a longcase clock*
a granny knot	"	*an unstable reef knot*
an old master painting	"	*a classic painting*
the Old Lady of Threadneedle Street	"	*the Bank of England*
a Johnny come lately	"	*an upstart*
Tom, Dick and Harry	"	*any ordinary person*

Recommendations to end the masculine tyranny of chess are even more controversial – or preposterous. Knights are to be renamed defenders or horseriders; kings become sovereigns and queens are deputy sovereigns.

Such bizarre examples should be ample warning to every aspiring writer. Be sensible and sensitive towards people and institutions, whether minorities or majorities, but say what you mean!

A word to the wise about Clichés

All things considered, avoid clichés like the plague

We have all met people who have the extraordinary ability to talk in clichés:

> Y'know, not to beat around the bush or hedge your bet, this chapter is a must-read because it calls a spade a spade and in a nutshell leaves no stone unturned to pull the rug from under those off-the-cuff, old-hat bête noires called clichés.

These are the people who've given the **cliché** its bad name. We all tend to use them, of course. Sometimes that familiar phrase is the neatest way of expressing yourself and most of us can, *in a flash* (cliché), unconsciously call up a few hundred of them to help us out in writing and conversation. But how aware are we of the irritation (or worse, sniggering) that the overuse of clichés can cause?

If you want to use clichés only when appropriate and, avoid them when not, it helps to be able to recognise them. Give yourself this quick test: how many of these tired and well-worn expressions can you complete with the missing word

COMPLETE THE CLICHÉ

1. *a gift from the . . . .*
2. *light at the end of the . . . . . .*
3. *weighed in the . . . . and found wanting*
4. *quantum . . . .*
5. *paper over the . . . . . .*
6. *fall between two . . . . . .*
7. *blot on the . . . .*
8. *if you've got it, ... it*
9. *the . . . . . not worth the candle*
10. *it's not over till the fat lady . . . . .*

Answers. 1. *gods*; 2. *tunnel*; 3. *balance*; 4. *leap*; 5. *cracks*; 6. *stools*; 7. *landscape*; 8. *flaunt*; 9. *game's*; 10. *sings*

Most clichés begin life as someone's incredibly neat, timely or witty way of expressing or emphasising a thought. Because it is clever, a lot of people steal the phrase as their own. Multiply that by a few million and you have the desperately tired and overused husk of somebody's originality.

Many clichés are centuries old. If we say of a jilted bride-to-be that she was *left in the lurch* we are echoing a comment made by the English poet Gabriel Harvey in 1576. Thirty years earlier saw another writer, John Heywood, recognise that he knew *what side his bread's buttered on* (1546). Clichés date from the Bible and more are minted, *waiting in the wings* (cliché) for clichédom, every day. These days a cliché can be born, adopted and be worn out in a matter of mere months.

The grammarian Eric Partridge identified four kinds of cliché. There is the idiom that becomes so indiscriminately used that its original meaning becomes lost (*to the manner born* has become *to the manor born* because of the widespread belief that it means born to wealth and luxury, whereas it originally meant 'following an established custom, or accustomed to a situation' as in Shakespeare's *Hamlet* 4:14). His second type includes phrases that have become so hackneyed that only the laziest writers and speakers ever use them (*to nip in the bud; beyond the pale; down to the last detail*).

Partridge's third group consists of foreign phrases (*terra firma; in flagrante delicto; plus ça change*) while his fourth comprises snippets and quotations from literature (*a little knowledge is a dangerous thing* from Pope, and Shakespeare's *a thing of beauty is a joy for ever*).

However we haven't yet rounded up *all the usual suspects* (cliché). One *serial offender* (very modern cliché) is the 'stock modifier' – a *Darby and Joan* (cliché) combination of words that, often for no reason, are always seen together. A person isn't moved; he or she is *visibly moved*; a person isn't merely courteous, he or she is *unfailingly courteous*. These parasitic partners are really sly clichés and you should watch for them. To help you know these partners better, try matching these:

1	*over-riding*	A	*consequences*
2	*woefully*	B	*apparent*
3	*far-reaching*	C	*inadequate*
4	*no-holds-barred*	D	*importance*
5	*increasingly*	E	*interview*

Answers: 1D; 2C; 3A; 4E; 5B

If you make up your mind to watch out for clichés creeping into your speech and writing and to try to avoid them you'll be surprised how easy it becomes to do without them – and how much fresher your writing becomes as a result.

Here are a few you might remove from your vocabulary:

An A to Z of Clichés to Avoid like the Plague

accidentally on purpose
accident waiting to happen
actions speak louder than words
act of contrition
acid test
add insult to injury
after due consideration
all intents and purposes
all in the same boat
all over bar the shouting
all things considered
almost too good to be true
angel of mercy
angry silence (classic *Darby & Joan*)
as a matter of fact
as luck would have it
as sure as eggs is/are eggs
at the end of the day
at this moment/point in time
auspicious occasion
avid reader

baby with the bathwater, don't throw out the
backseat driver
back to basics/to the drawing board
bag and baggage
bag of tricks
ballpark figure
ball's in your court, the
bang your head against a brick wall
barking up the wrong tree
bat an eyelid (try *wink* and surprise everyone)
batten down the hatches
beavering away
beer and skittles, it's not all
before you can say Jack Robinson
beggars can't be choosers
be good (and if you can't be good, be careful!)

be that as it may
between a rock and a hard place
bite the bullet
blessing in disguise
blind leading the blind
blissful ignorance
blood out of a stone, it's like trying to get
bloody but unbowed
blow hot and cold
blot on the landscape
blow the whistle
blue rinse brigade
blushing bride
bone of contention
borrowed time
bottom line
breath of fresh air
bright eyed and bushy tailed
brought to book
brownie points
bruising battle/encounter
bumper to bumper traffic jam
by the same token

call it a day
callow youth
calm before the storm
camp as a row of tents
can of worms
captive audience
card up his sleeve
cards stacked against us
cardinal sin
carte blanche
cast of thousands
Catch 22 situation
catalogue of errors/misery/disaster/misfortune
cat among the pigeons, put the
catholic tastes
caustic comment
cautious optimism
centre of the universe

chalk and cheese, as different as
champing at the bit
chapter and verse
chapter of accidents
cheek by jowl
cheque's in the post, the
cheap and cheerful
cherished belief
chew the cud/fat
chop and change
chorus of approval/dispproval
chosen few
circumstances beyond our control
cold light of day, in the
cold water on, pour
come home to roost
comes to the crunch, when it
common or garden
compulsive viewing/reading
conspicious by his/her absence
cool as a cucumber
cool, calm and collected
copious notes (and, if made by a reporter, usually *scribbled notes*)
crack of dawn
crazy like a fox
crème de la crème
crisis of confidence
cross that bridge when we come to it, we'll
cry over spilt milk
current climate, in the
cut a long story short, to
cut and dried
cut any ice, it doesn't/won't
cutting edge

damn with faint praise
Darby and Joan
darkest hour is just before dawn
dark secret
day in, day out
dead as a dodo
dead in the water

deadly accurate
dead of night, in the
dead to the world
deafening silence
deaf to entreaties
death's door, at
death warmed up, like
depths of depravity
desert a sinking ship
despite misgivings
devour every word (and then there are none left to *hang on to*)
dicing with death
dim and distant past, in the
dog eat dog
donkey's years ago, it was
don't call us, we'll call you
don't count your chickens before they're hatched
doom and gloom merchants
dot the i's and cross the t's
drop of a hat, at the
dry as a bone
dyed in the wool

each and everyone
eager beaver
eagerly devour
ear to the ground
easier said than done
eat humble pie
eat your heart out
economical with the truth
empty nest, empty nesters, empty nest syndrome
enfant terrible
eternal regret/ eternal shame, to my
every dog has his day
every man jack of them
everything but the kitchen sink
every little helps
every stage of the game, at
explore every avenue

face the facts/music
fact of the matter, the

fair and square
fair sex, the
fall between two stools/by the wayside
fall on deaf ears
far and wide
far be it from me
fast and furious
fast lane, in the
fate worse than death
feel-good factor, the
few and far between
field day, having a
fighting fit
final insult
fine-tooth comb, go/went through it with a
finger in every pie
finger of suspicion
firing on all cylinders
first and foremost
first things first
fish out of water
fit as a fiddle
fits and starts, in/by
flash in the pan
flat as a pancake
flat denial
flavour of the month
flog a dead horse
fly in the ointment
fond belief
food for thought
footloose and fancy free
forlorn hope
fraught with danger/peril
free, gratis and for nothing
frenzy of activity
from the sublime to the ridiculous
from the word go
fudge the issue
fullness of time, in the
funny ha-ha or funny peculiar?
F-word

gainful employment
gameplan
generous to a fault
gentle giant
gentleman's agreement
gentler sex, the
girl Friday
give a dog a bad name
give him an inch and he'll take a yard
give up the ghost
glowing tribute
glutton for punishment
goes without saying, it
goes from strength to strength
golden opportunity
good as gold
go off half-cocked
gory details, the
grasp the nettle
greatest thing since sliced bread
great unwashed, the
green with envy
grim death, like
grin and bear it
grind/ground to a halt
grist to the mill
guardian angel

hale and hearty
hand in glove with
handle with kid gloves
hand over fist
hand to mouth existence
handwriting is on the wall
hanged for a sheep as a lamb, we might as well be
happy accident/event/hunting ground/medium
happily ensconced
hard and fast rule
has what it takes
having said that
have a nice one
have got a lot on my plate, I've

have I got news for you?
head and shoulders above
heaping ridicule
heart and soul
heart's in the right place, his/her
hell or high water
high and dry
hit or miss
hit the nail on the head
hit the panic button
hive of activity
Hobson's choice
hold your horses
hoist with his own petard
honest truth, the
hope against hope
horns of a dilemma, on the
horses for courses
howling gale
how long is a piece of string?
how time flies

If *the worst comes to the worst*
if you can't beat 'em, join 'em
if you can't stand the heat get out of the kitchen
if you've got it, flaunt it
ignorance is bliss
ill-gotten gains
ill-starred venture
impossible dream, an/the
in all conscience/honesty
in a nutshell
inch-by-inch search
in less than no time
in one ear and out the other
inordinate amount of
in the pipeline
in this day and age
iota, not one
it never rains but it pours
it's a small world
it's not the end of the world

it stands to reason
it will all come out in the wash
it will all end in tears
it will soon blow over
ivory tower

jack of all trades (but master of none)
jaundiced eye
jewel in the crown
Johnny-come-lately
jockey for position
jump on the bandwagon
jump the gun
just deserts
just for the record
just what the doctor ordered

keep a low profile
keep a straight face
keep my/your head above water
keep the wolf from the door
keep your chin up
keep your nose clean
keep your nose to the grindstone
kickstart
kill two birds with one stone
kill with kindness
kiss of death
knee-high to a grasshopper
knocked into a cocked hat
knocked/knocks the spots off
know the ropes
know which side your bread's buttered on
knuckle under

labour of love
lack-lustre performance
lap of luxury
large as life/larger than life
last but not least
last straw, it's the
late in the day
laugh all the way to the bank

laugh up your sleeve
lavish praise/hospitality/ceremony
lay it on with a trowel
leading light
leave/left in the lurch
leave no stone unturned (or as the bird hater said, *leave no tern unstoned*)
let bygones be bygones
let's get this show on the road
let sleeping dogs lie
let well alone
lick his/their wounds
level playing field
light at the end of the tunnel
like a house on fire
little the wiser
little woman
live and let live
local difficulty, a little
lock, stock and barrel
long arm of the law
long hot summer
long time no see
loose end, at a
lost cause
lost in admiration
lost in contemplation
love you and leave you, I must

made of sterner stuff
made/make a killing
make a mountain out of a molehill
make an offer I can't refuse
make ends meet
make hay while the sun shines
make no bones about it
make my day
make or break
make/making short work of it
make/making the best of a bad job
make/making tracks
man after my own heart, a
make/making waves

manna from heaven
man of straw/man of the world
man to man
many hands make light work
mark my words
matter of life and death
method in his madness
Midas touch, the
millstone around your neck
mind boggles, the
mixed blessing (and a variation, *it was not an unmixed blessing . . .*)
model of its kind/propriety
moment of truth
moot point
more haste, less speed
more in sorrow than in anger
more than meets the eye
more the merrier, the
mortgaged to the hilt
movers and shakers
move the goalposts
much-needed reforms
much of a muchness
muddy the waters
mutton dressed as lamb

nail in his coffin, put/drive a
name of the game, the
nearest and dearest
necessity is the mother of invention
neck and neck
needle in a haystack
needless to say
neither here nor there
new lease of life
nick of time, in the
nine-day/day's wonder
nip it in the bud/nipped in the bud
nitty-gritty
no expense spared
no names, no pack drill
no news is good news

no peace for the wicked
no problem
no skin off my nose
no spring chicken
nothing to write home about
nothing ventured, nothing gained
not just a pretty face
not out of the woods yet
not to be sneezed at
not to put too fine a point on it
now or never

odd man out
odds and ends
off the beaten track
off the cuff
old as the hills
older and wiser
once bitten, twice shy
once in a blue moon
one fell swoop
one in a million
only time will tell
on the ball
on the level
on the spur of the moment
on the tip of my tongue
out of sight, out of mind
out of the blue
out on a limb
over and done with
over my dead body
over the top
own goal, score an
own worst enemy

packed in like sardines
painstaking investigation
pale into insignificance
palpable nonsense
paper over the cracks
par for the course
part and parcel

pass muster
past its/his/her sell-by date
patter of tiny feet
pay through your nose
pecking order
picture of health
piece de resistance
pie in the sky
pinpoint accuracy
plain as a pikestaff
plain as the nose on your face
play your cards right
pleased as Punch
point of no return
poisoned chalice
pound of flesh
powers that be, the
practice makes perfect
press on regardless
pride and joy
pride of place
proof of the pudding
pull out all the stops
pure as the driven snow
put on hold/the back burner
put two and two together
put up or shut up
put your best foot forward
put your foot down
put your money where your mouth is
put your nose out of joint

quality of life
quantum leap
queer the pitch
quick and the dead
quid pro quo
quiet before the storm, the

race against time
rack and ruin, going to
raining cats and dogs (and hailing taxis)
rat race, the

read my lips
red rag to a bull, like a
reinventing the wheel
reliable source (the reporter's friend)
resounding silence
right as rain
rings a bell
rings true
risk life and limb
rock the boat, don't
Rome wasn't built in a day
rose by any other name, a
rotten apple in a barrel, one
rough diamond, a
ruffled feathers
ruled with a rod of iron
run it up the flagpole (and see who salutes)
run of the mill
run to seed

safe and sound
sailing close to the wind
sale of the century
salt of the earth
saved by the bell
search high and low
second to none
seething cauldron
see eye to eye
see how the land lies
see the wood for the trees, can't
sell like hot cakes
serial gossiper/meddler/bullshit artist etc
serious money
set in stone/concrete
shape or form, in any
share and share alike
ships that pass in the night
shoot yourself in the foot/ shot himself in the foot
short and sweet
shot across the bows
sick and tired

sick as a parrot
sight for sore eyes
signed, sealed and delivered
silent majority, the
simmering hatred
sitting duck
sixes and sevens
six of one and half-a-dozen of the other
skating on thin ice
skin of his teeth
slaving over a hot stove all day, I've been
slowly but surely
smell a rat
snatch defeat from the jaws of victory (and, of course, vice versa!)
so far so good
solid as a rock
so near and yet so far
sorely needed
sour grapes
splendid isolation
square peg in a round hole
straight and narrow, stick to the
straight from the shoulder
strange as it may seem/ strange to relate
strike while the iron's hot
suffer fools gladly, he/she doesn't
suffer in silence
survival of the fittest
sugar the pill
sweetness and light, all
swept off his feet
swings and roundabouts

tail between his legs, he went off with his
take it with a grain of salt
take the bull by the horns
take the rough with the smooth
tarred with the same brush
teach your mother/grandmother to suck eggs
technological wizardry
teething troubles
tender loving care (TLC)

tender mercies
terra firma
thankful for small mercies, be
that's life
that's the way the cookie crumbles
there but for the grace of God go I
thereby hangs a tale
there's no such thing as a free lunch
this day and age
throw in the towel
thunderous applause
tighten our/your belts
time flies

time heals everything/ all ills
time waits for no man
tip of the iceberg, the
tired and emotional
tireless campaigner/crusader
tissue of lies
to all intents and purposes
tomorrow is another day
too little, too late
to my dying day
too awful/terrible/horrible to contemplate
too many cooks (spoil the broth)
too numerous to mention
torrential rain
towering inferno
tower of strength
trials and tribulations
turn a deaf ear
turn over a new leaf
twenty-twenty hindsight
twinkling of an eye, in a
twisted him around her little finger
two's company, three's a crowd

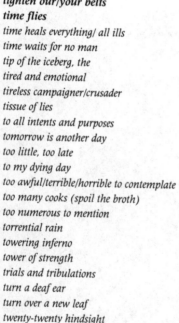

ultra-sophisticated
unacceptable face of capitalism (or any other institution you want to knock)
unavoidable delay
unalloyed delight
unconscionable time, taking an/unconscionable liar

under a cloud
under the weather
unequal task
university of life
unkindest cut of all
unsung heroes
untimely end
untold wealth
unvarnished truth
up to scratch/not up to scratch
upper crust

vanish into thin air
variety is the spice of life
vested interest
vicious circle
vote with their feet

wages of sin (is death)
waited on hand and foot
walking on air/eggs
walking on broken glass
warts and all
waste not, want not
water under the bridge
wealth of experience/material/knowledge
wedded bliss
weighed in the balance and found wanting
well-earned rest
wheels within wheels
when the cats away the mice will play
when the going gets tough (the tough get going)
whiter than white
winter of discontent
with all due respect
with bated breath
with malice aforethought
without a shadow of a doubt
without fear of contradiction
woman scorned, hell hath no fury like a
wonders will never cease
word to the wise, a
work my fingers to the bone, I

world's your oyster, the
writing's on the wall, the
wrong end of the stick, you've got the

yawning gulf
year in, year out
you can bet your bottom dollar/last penny
you can lead a horse to water but you can't make him drink
you can't make a silk purse out of a sow's ear
you can't teach an old dog new tricks
you can't win 'em all
you could have knocked me down with a feather
you get what you pay for
you pays your money and takes your choice
your guess is as good as mine
you're breaking my heart
you're only young once

What's your cliché rating?

How many clichés, worn-out phrases and stale proverbs from that list are you aware of having written lately?

● **MORE THAN TEN?**
If there were such a person as a cliché-holic, it would be you. If your job involves much writing, someone in the office could be making a secret collection of your greatest excesses. For penance, study the list again and promise yourself a thorough cliché clear-out.

● **BETWEEN FIVE AND TEN?**
You are not a hopeless case – yet. But do run a cliché detector over your next piece of writing before you let anyone see it.

● **UP TO FIVE?**
Not bad – but don't slacken. If five clichés can get past you, so can six, seven . . . and before you know it you'll be standing in Cliché Corner wearing *the dunce's cap* (unlisted cliché).

● **NOT A SINGLE ONE?**
Almost *too good to be true* (cliché). But if you're sure you are not even slightly cheating, congratulations on helping to keep the English language fresh and alive!

Clarity Begins at Home: How to improve your powers of expression

Circumambulate the Non-representational: Avoid the Abstract

Humans are of the type of matter that constitutes dreams and their relatively brief existences terminate, as well as taking their inception, in a state of unconsciousness.

William Shakespeare, *The Tempest*, IV, i

Shakespeare? Never! Well, yes, but not quite. The quote is from Prospero's retort to Ferdinand, the son of the King of Naples, in *The Tempest*:

We are such stuff
As dreams are made on, and our little life
Is rounded with a sleep

. . . except that it was rewritten by Oxford University Professor Richard Gombrich to parody the overblown, tedious writing style of many literary editors and critics.

Sentences consist of many parts of speech (which we'll discuss later) but will almost certainly include one or more nouns. And, again, there are several kinds of nouns, but the two kinds which concern us here are **concrete nouns** and **abstract nouns**.

A concrete noun is something that is perceptible, tangible – something real that you can touch and see and smell: *wood, table, hair, blood*. An abstract noun refers to ideas, concepts, qualities, states of mind: *beauty, fascism, doubt, truth, fear*. Using one without care can knock the stuffing out of what you are trying to express. But there is nothing wrong with the words themselves when used properly.

Aspect, for example, is correctly used to mean the way in which a landscape, a problem or a situation may be viewed: *When looked at from the aspect of Britain's interests the proposal is unsatisfactory*. But when the word is used to mean part or consideration, a sentence can suddenly become soggy: *The government must consider the economic aspect.* Readers' minds always have to work harder when confronted by abstract nouns, adverbial and adjectival phrases.

Look again at our Shakespearean re-write and note the abstract nouns: *type, matter, existences, inception, unconsciousness.* They outnumber the concrete nouns (*humans, dreams*) by two to one, and as a result you have a sentence that can send the reader's brain into a spin trying to work out the meaning. Shakespeare's original text, even though expressed in antique prose, is much simpler to grasp.

The novelist and playwright Keith Waterhouse found Lincoln's Gettysburg Address to be a model of balance between abstract and concrete nouns. The President's speech is all about abstract, philosophical thoughts which a lot of us would have trouble understanding. But Lincoln solved the problem by anchoring to simple things that most people could readily understand. The passage is well worth studying as an exercise in the intelligent use of abstract and concrete nouns. In the speech the concrete nouns are highlighted in bold type, and the abstract nouns are underlined:

> *Fourscore and seven <u>years</u> ago our **fathers** brought forth on this*
> ***continent** a new **nation** conceived in <u>liberty</u> and dedicated to the*
> *<u>proposition</u> that all **men** are created equal. Now we are engaged in a*
> *great civil <u>war</u> testing whether that **nation**, or any **nation** so conceived*
> *and so dedicated, can long endure. We are met on a great **battlefield** of*
> *that <u>war</u>. We have come to dedicate a <u>portion</u> of that **field** as a final*
> ***resting-place** for those who here gave their <u>lives</u> that that **nation***
> *might live. It is altogether fitting and proper that we should do this.*
> *But, in a larger <u>sense</u>, we cannot dedicate, we cannot consecrate, we*
> *cannot hallow this **ground**. The brave **men**, living and dead, who*
> *struggled here have consecrated it far above our poor <u>power</u> to add or*
> *detract. The **world** will little note or long remember what we say here,*
> *but it can never forget what they did here. It is for us the **living** rather*
> *to be dedicated here to the unfinished <u>work</u> which they who fought here*
> *have thus far so nobly advanced. It is rather for us to be here dedicated*
> *to the great <u>task</u> remaining before us – that from these honoured **dead***
> *we take increased <u>devotion</u> to that <u>cause</u> for which they gave the last full*
> *measure of <u>devotion</u> – that we here highly resolve that these **dead** shall*
> *not have died in vain, that this **nation** under <u>God</u> shall have a new*
> *<u>birth</u> of <u>freedom</u>, and that <u>government</u> of the **people**, by the **people**, for*
> *the **people**, shall not perish from the **earth**.*

You can easily see how the 18 abstract nouns expressing ideas and concepts (*liberty, power, devotion, God*, etc) are brought down to earth – and understanding – by the 21 concrete nouns (*nation, men, resting-place, the people*, etc).

If, on re-reading something you've written you find it a bit tortuous, a bit difficult to follow, the fault may lie in your over-use of abstract nouns. So look at your piece again, identify the culprits, and try to do without them.

Here is a short list of everyday abstract nouns and adjective/adverb phrases with suggestions on how they might be replaced.

Some Awful Abstracts

(in) abeyance – in *the fitness classes were **in abeyance**.* Try *the fitness classes were suspended/interrupted/discontinued.*

amenity – as in *the school has gymnasium and swimming **amenities**.* Try *the school has a gymnasium and swimming pool.*

aspect – as in *the major **aspect** of the campaign.* Try *the important part of the plan.*

attitude – as in *he adopted a menacing **attitude**.* Try *he looked menacing.*

availability – as in *supplies will be subject to limited **availability**.* Try *supplies will be limited/scarce.*

basis – as in *she worked on a part-time **basis**.* Try *she worked part-time.* This word can sensibly be used when it really means basis: a foundation, a beginning, or main ingredient, as in *the general marshalled his troops on the basis of the spy's information; the basis of their romance was a shared love of music.*

capability, capacity – as in *Iraq has a chemical warfare **capability/capacity**.* Try *Iraq has chemical weapons.*

cessation – as in *a **cessation** of hostilities was hoped for.* Try *it was hoped hostilities would end/cease/stop.*

character – as in *the parcel was of a suspect **character**.* Try *the parcel was suspect.*

degree – as in *she displayed a high **degree** of restraint.* Try *she showed great restraint.*

description – as in *they had no plans of any **description**.* Try *they had no plans.*

desirability – as in *he questioned the **desirability** of the proposals.* Try *he sked whether the proposals were desirable.*

element – as in *there was a rebel **element** in the village.* Try *there were rebels in the village.*

expectation – as in *the government's **expectation** was for an optimistic outcome.* Try *the government expected an optimistic outcome.*

factor – as in *don't forget the unemployment **factor**.* Try *don't forget unemployment.*

level – as in *the general **level** of conduct was satisfactory.* Try *generally/in general, conduct was satisfactory.*

manner – as in *he drove in a reckless **manner**.* Try *he drove recklessly.*

nature – as in *they made arrangements of a temporary **nature**.* Try *they made temporary arrangements.*

operation – as in *the automatic doors were not in **operation**.* Try *the automatic doors were not working.*

participation – as in *there was enthusiastic **participation** on the part of the members.* Try *the members took part enthusiastically.*

persuasion – as in *Joyce was of the strict Methodist **persuasion**.* Try *Joyce was a strict Methodist.*

situation – as in *please let me know about the present state of the **situation**.* Try *please let me know how things are/stand.*

Overloading can sink your sentence

We recommend an average sentence length of 15-25 words to make any text easy to read.

Plain English Campaign

By now, if you have been eliminating euphemism, jettisoning jargon, cutting out clichés and showing the gate to gobblegook, your writing should be looking leaner and meaner. But there still remains a curious human impulse to overcome: the tendency to let the moving finger write, and write, and write . . . on and on. In short, to pack as much into a sentence as possible.

Consider this passage from the *Daily Telegraph*:

Seven of the 33 buildings in St James's Square, in the heart of one of the most expensive parts of London, display For Sale or To Let signs.

Nothing wrong there. But then:

The sight of some of the capital's most exclusive business addresses languishing empty – when not long ago they were snapped up as corporate headquarters – brings home the impact of the recession as financial controllers cut costs by letting out spare space vacated by staff who have been made redundant or exiled to less costly locations.

Now, readers of the national 'quality' newspapers may be perfectly able to to wind their way through that sentence. But why should they have to?

Let's count the items of information that the author has loaded in:

1.   *some of the capital's most exclusive business addresses*
2.   *are empty*
3.   *when not long ago they were snapped up*
4.   *as corporate headquarters*
5.   *impact of the recession*
6.   *financial controllers cutting costs*
7.   *by letting out spare space*

8.   *. . . which was left empty when staff either were made redundant*
9.   *or moved*
10.   *to somewhere cheaper*

Clearly, the structure of this overloaded sentence ought to be dismantled and reassembled in a more manageable form. The major items of information are:

(a)   the situation is caused by an economic recession;

(b)   the recession meant that offices were emptied because staff were sacked or moved to cheaper accommodation;

(c)   companies also saved money by renting out offices they once occupied themselves.

What could the author have done instead? Well, he or she could have written:

The sight of some of the capital's most exclusive business addresses languishing empty brings home the impact of the recession. Offices have been left empty as staff were made redundant, or moved to cheaper accommodation. Financial controllers have cut costs by letting out the space their firms no longer need.

Overloaded sentences do not have to be long. Here's one with an unremarkable 47 words but it is still well above the Plimsoll Line of saturated sentences:

A man living alone was approaching his house when he was attacked by seven armed robbers who forced him at gunpoint to open the front door of his secluded country cottage in Kent before leaving him so badly beaten that he is now afraid to return home.

The main news points in this opening sentence seem to be:

(a)   a man was badly beaten by robbers in his secluded cottage in Kent;

(b)   he was beaten so badly that he is now afraid to return home – presumably from hospital.

The additional facts – that he was approaching his house when the attack took place, that there were seven robbers, that they were armed, that they forced him at gunpoint to open the front door, can wait a moment. The vital principle in a story like this is to put the main facts first. And if you think there are just too many facts for a single sentence, turn it into two sentences:

A man living alone in a secluded cottage in Kent was beaten so badly by robbers that he is afraid to go home. Seven armed men struck as he approached the house, and forced him at gunpoint to open his front door.

Even though we now have two sentences, we have managed to save five words. But more importantly, the reading task is easier and the meaning is clearer.

Nowhere is overloading more pronounced than in bureaucratic documents – they are so weighed down with circumlocution, jargon and gobbledegook.

Here's a typical passage from a booklet called Frameworks for the Future, about the Northern Ireland settlement proposals. It won the 1994 Golden Rhubarb Trophy for the most confusing government document of the year:

> *Where either government considers that any institution, established as part of the overall accommodation, is not properly functioning within the Agreement or that a breach of the Agreement has otherwise occurred, the Conference shall consider the matter on the basis of a shared commitment to arrive at a common position or, where that is not possible, to agree a procedure to resolve the difference between them.*

You should have quickly spotted some Awful Abstract nouns in this 66-word sentence (*breach, matter, basis, commitment, procedure*) and sensed that there are far too many facts and thoughts in it for comfortable digestion. Let's see if we can render it in plain English in a single sentence:

> *If either government feels that any institutions established by the Agreement are not working properly, or breaching the Agreement, the Conference will try to find a common position or agree a procedure to resolve any differences.*

This version seems to retain the intended meaning of the original and at 36 words is shorter and clearer. But a 36-word sentence is still suspect (remember the Plain English Campaign's recommended 25-25 words). So let us try again, this time with two sentences:

> *The governments may feel that institutions established by the Agreement are either not working properly or breaching the Agreement. In such cases the Conference will try to find either a common position or a procedure that will resolve any differences.*

We've used four more words than the single-sentence rewrite, but the meaning sticks out a mile. If any proof were needed that shorter sentences help understanding, this exercise should have provided it.

The no-no non sequitur

A common feature of many overlong, overweight sentences is the presence of non sequiturs. A non sequitur is a statement that has little or no relevance to what preceded it – a sentence that attempts to join the unjoinable:

> *the egg-and-spoon race was won by Julia Jones whose parents taught her to sing and tap dance.*

You might well ask, what does singing and tap dancing have to do with winning an egg-and-spoon race? That is a non sequitur. These are usually caused by a writer's hankering to compress information with a minimum of punctuation, but the inevitable consequence is confusion:

> *Mr Pearson was a star graduate of the University of Birmingham's highly regarded science faculty and he travelled widely throughout Eastern Europe as a part-time tennis instructor.*

Although fairly short this sentence still suffers from overload – in this case two quite different, even opposing, sets of facts:

(a) Mr Pearson was a star science graduate from Birmingham University

(b) He was a part-time tennis instructor in Eastern Europe

If the two sets of facts were relevant to each other, the problem wouldn't exist:

> *Mr Pearson was a star graduate of the University of Birmingham's highly regarded science faculty, and he quickly found a high-paying position with ICI.*

In other words he quickly found a job because he was a star graduate. Or the second set of facts might be related to the first because they were surprising:

> *Mr Pearson was a star graduate of the University of Birmingham's highly regarded science faculty despite his having no previous grounding in any science subjects.*

Here we have no trouble with the two sets of facts because they are joined (*despite*) by a common interest.

But returning to our original example, if the two sets of facts about Mr Pearson are all we have, we could remove the *and* separating *faculty* and *he* to form two sentences. But they would be irritatingly short – and still confusingly irrelevant to each other. If you are faced with a situation like this your options are so limited that a rewrite is probably the best way out. For example:

> *After leaving the University of Birmingham's highly regarded science faculty as a star graduate, Mr Pearson decided to to travel throughout Eastern Europe as a tennis instructor.*

To avoid overload, re-read and rewrite. Or as someone once said – but not about over-long sentences – divide and conquer.

Avoiding the minefield of Muddle

Any person not placing dog litter in this receptacle will be liable to a fine of £100.

Sign in Kensington Gardens

If, walking in the park without a dog and lacking any dog litter (or for that matter, dogshit), would we be required to search for some to deposit in the bin to avoid the £100 fine?

That ambiguous sentence is the victim of muddled thinking and, consequently, muddled writing. There's a lot of it about. Perhaps it's because we're trained in logical leapfrog by a diet of newspaper headlines:

Police Discover Crack in Devon
MARS BARS PROTEST
Milk Drinkers Are Turning To Powder
VIRGIN TAKES RECORD BOOKINGS
General Flies Back To Front
POLICE FIND CONSTABLE DRAWING IN ATTIC

Most people can translate muddled mind-benders like those without even thinking. Longer passages, however, can cause momentary confusion:

The witness told the commissioners that she had seen sexual intercourse taking place between two parked cars in front of her house.

US newspaper report

You can't imagine how out of things I feel, never to be able to discuss how my husband hasn't touched me in months, the way all my girlfriends do.

letter to a women's magazine agony column

Not all such muddled writing is funny; most of it is simply confusing, irritating and, in some cases, potentially harmful. But it all has a common origin: muddled writing occurs when the author is not really thinking about what he or she is putting on paper.

Disaster at lunchtime

The lunch hour is not what it appears to be for the majority of workers.
An hour is more likely to be fewer than 30 minutes for two in every five workers, while a mere 5 per cent take a more leisurely attitude and admit to exceeding the traditional time limit.

The Independent

The apparent attempt at being jokey turns the first part of paragraph two into a muddle of statistics likely to dissuade most readers from finishing the sentence.

Mixing ordinary numbers with percentages is another annoyance; the reader has to stop and try to work out how the two sets of statistics (two in every five; 5 per cent) compare. But perhaps the passage can be rescued:

For 40 in every 100 workers, that 'hour' is likely to be under 30 minutes. Only five in 100 take a more leisurely attitude and admit to exceeding the traditional time limit.

An ugly mess in the vestibule

The high for the day was achieved for a marble Georgian chimney-piece circa 1770 with superbly carved tablets of Diana and her hounds. It went on estimate for £23,650 to Bartlett, the Bermondsey dealer in architectural fittings who paid £330 for three piles of marble at Castle Howard last year which he has since sold to America for about £150,000, reconstructed as a 15ft vestibule by Sir John Vanbrugh.

Eaton Hall Estate auction report in the *Daily Telegraph*

This is a thorough mess, breathtakingly muddled. Ignoring the jargonaut's *high* in the first sentence, we are violently wrenched from the latest doings of Bermondsey Bartlett to an entirely different event, year and place.

What exactly was it that Bartlett from Bermondsey 'sold to America'? The marble? Castle Howard? Last year itself? Did he sell it to the American Government? And what exactly was reconstructed as a 15ft vestibule by Sir John Vanbrugh? Marble? Castle Howard?

And wasn't Sir John Vanbrugh, by then, rather old to be reconstructing anything, having died in 1726?

With a minimum of research we find that Sir John was an architect besides being a playwright. Castle Howard, in Yorkshire, was the first building he designed. So could it be that the three piles of marble had originally been a

15ft vestibule which he'd designed? If we assume it is, it now becomes possible, with heavy lifting-gear and wearing our hard hats, to reconstruct this pile of literary rubble – not, perhaps, as a grand 15ft vestibule, but at least as a piece of clear English:

> . . . It went at the estimated price, £23,650, to Bartlett, the Bermondsey dealer in architectural fittings. Last year, at Castle Howard, the same dealer paid £330 for three piles of marble, originally a 15ft vestibule by the castle's architect, Sir John Vanbrugh. Bartlett has since sold the marble in America for around £150,000, where it has been used to reconstruct the vestibule.

And not a scrap of Vanbrugh's valuable verbal marble vandalised!

Doorstep body horror

This absurdity, taken from an American newspaper, is a masterpiece of muddle:

> A Texan undertaker left the body of a man on the doorstep of his son because he could not afford a cremation.

Let's try to decode this one. Whose son owned the doorstep? The dead man's son? The undertaker's son? Who could not afford a cremation? The dead man? His son? The undertaker?

At first sight, this dreadful sentence (in other circumstances it would deserve the adjective *deathless* = immortal) appears easy to rewrite without confusion or any loss of meaning. But try doing it also without repetition, which the writer may have been desperate to avoid:

> A Texan undertaker dumped a dead man on the man's son's doorstep because the son could not afford a cremation.

Although the meaning is now quite clear the sentence is clumsy and repetitive. It's worth another try:

> A dead man was dumped on his son's doorstep by a Texan undertaker because the son could not afford a cremation.

Again, the facts are crystal clear but the sentence is still repetitive. Another try:

> A dead man whose son could not afford a cremation was dumped on the son's doorstep by a Texan undertaker.

Many writers would settle for this version but perfectionists would recognise that the order of facts is a bit muddled. And it still repeats *son*, perhaps unnecessarily. It's worth a final shot, but this time let's take a small liberty by introducing the word *family* which in this context would be acceptable usage:

A Texan undertaker who found that a dead man's family could not afford a cremation dumped the body on the son's doorstep.

To visit, or not to visit?

Trust staff, the report discloses, have been advised that they should only visit the area after midday in the event of an emergency.

What can this snippet mean? It could be saying: *Trust staff have been advised that if there is an emergency, they should not visit the area in the morning.* But it could also be saying: *Trust staff have been advised that the only time to visit the area is after midday – and even then, only if there is an emergency.*

If we look closely at the original sentence we can narrow the search for the source of confusion to the word *only*, or rather its placing. Does the writer mean only visit that area? Or visit that area only after midday? Or visit after midday only if there is an emergency?

There is also another problem which adds to the confusion: the piece of verbiage, *in the event of*, meaning, in clearer English, *if there is* or *unless there is an emergency*.

What the sentence so clumsily failed to convey was this:

Trust staff have been advised not to visit the area after midday, unless there is an emergency.

When you use *only*, make sure that you have it in the right place. *Professor Hawking only published his book after years of deep thought.* Does this mean that all the Professor ever did was to publish this one book? It seems so, but it's not true. What the sentence intended to convey was *Professor Hawking published his book only after years of deep thought.* When using the adverb *only* in circumstances like these, ensure that it is placed next to the word it modifies.

Like as not

Another source of muddle and obscurity is the word *like*. One of the most common ways in which *like* is misused is to introduce examples:

It included stars like Frank Sinatra, Bob Hope and Michael Jackson.

Who were these lookalikes? Or do we really mean *stars such as*? Fortunately this form of misuse is so common that it rarely causes misunderstanding.

*My mother can't get through a busy day **like** (as) she used to; It sounded **like** (as if, as though) she was about to scream the house down; **Like** (Just as) in Pam's case, Liz received no compensation* are examples of *like* used as an all-purpose conjunction. When using it read the sentence over carefully; in many cases your 'ear' will warn you of possible misuse.

Might or may

The misuse of *may* instead of *might* is also common and can confuse. *May* is correct when an outcome is still unknown. *Might* is right when an *if* is lurking in the background – when we discuss something that was likely or possible on some past occasion.

RIGHT: *If it had not been for the paramedics, I **might** have died. (but I didn't)*
WRONG: *If it had not been for the paramedics, I **may** have died.*
RIGHT: *I accept that I **may** have been mistaken. (I am still not sure)*
WRONG: *I accept that I **might** have been mistaken.*
RIGHT: *It **might** have been a mistake to turn right, so I didn't. (at the time I wasn't sure)*
WRONG: *It **might** have been a mistake to turn right, because I finished up hitting another car.*
RIGHT: *It **may** have been a mistake, but I turned right. (I still don't know whether it was a mistake or not)*
WRONG: *It **may** have been a mistake to turn right, so I didn't.*

Remember to use *may* in the present and future tense; *might* in the past. *The boss **may** leave for New York tomorrow; The boss **might** have left last night.*

Danglers and floaters

These are the somewhat colourful descriptions for what are more boringly known as **unattached** or **hanging participles**. You may not be familiar with the technical term and you may not immediately recognise them, but you have probably experienced the head scratching they cause when you come across them in print:

After the first day, sleeping after a 1,000 ft climb, my underpants were eaten by warrior ants.

In recounting his trip to the Andes, The Times columnist Matthew Parris upstages the scenery when he introduces us to his incredible underpants, with their ability to climb mountains and sleep. Millions would have paid good money to see these but unfortunately they succumbed to an attack by warrior ants.

Danglers like that one can often be found somewhere in the middle of a muddled passage, of which this is a typical example:

However, the optimistic forecasts by the societies have repeatedly been disappointed over the past few years and they are again having to admit that the market is still on its back.

Richard Thomson in *The Observer*

Well, we get the drift, so it's not seriously ambiguous, but why should part of our minds gave to grapple with forecasts that appear to possess the human abilities to be disappointed, and to make admissions?

And how can you suppress the exotic, Dali-esque and distracting mind-picture evoked by the blurb on this book jacket:

> *She lives in London with a large Scotsman, their daughters Georgia and Holly, a nanny and a goldfish, where she now writes full time.*

As with many other traps waiting to trip us up and muddle our prose, danglers and their like can be avoided by the following ways:

- **Take some time to think out what you want to say before you begin to write**

- **While you are writing, test your prose phrase by phrase, sentence by sentence, to make sure you are expressing exactly what you want to say**

- **When you have finished, re-read every sentence carefully and ensure that nothing can be misunderstood.**

Measuring the murk with the FOG Index

The Fog Index is probably the most useful measuring stick for turgidity in writing.

American lexicographer David Grambs

We've now looked at the principal factors that contribute to poor communication, confusion, long-windedness and plain bad writing. Their presence or absence determines whether a piece of writing will be readable or not. Even if you are an eloquent stylist and have all your grammar correct, the readability of what you write will be demolished by the evils of circumlocution, gobbledegook, jargon, overloading and muddle. Readability, to put it plainly, is what good writing is all about.

Can you measure readability? Well, not precisely. But a method has been devised that provides a rough yardstick to tell if a written passage will be read and understood with ease. It's called the **Fog Index**.

The Fog Index was invented by an American anti-jargon, pro-clarity crusader named Robert Gunning. The Index runs from a factor of around 7 (clear and precise) to 15 and above (considered impenetrable); a Fog Index of 13 or over is a warning that the writer may have made the going unnecessarily heavy for the reader.

However its inventor is at pains to point out that the Fog Index is not a template to work with when you write – and it is fallible. Rather, it is a useful tool for measuring comprehensibility and deciding whether a piece of writing is suitable for its intended readership. So treat the Fog Index as a semi-serious check on the clarity of what you have written.

How the Fog Index works

1. Choose a section of the written work, at least 100 words long. Count the exact number of words.

2. Count the number of sentences. If a long sentence contains two or more complete thoughts, separated by commas, colons or semi-colons, treat each thought as a sentence.

3.   Divide the total number of words by the total number of sentences. That will give you the average sentence length.

4.   Now go through the same passage, counting the number of words of three or more syllables. Ignore proper names, words that are combinations of short, easy words (such as *caretaker, bookkeeper, headmaster*) and words which are of three syllables because an *-ed, -s,* or *-es* has been added to the basic word (like *invent-ed, transpose-s*).

5.   Now (getting out your calculator would be wise at this point) find the percentage of multi-syllable words by dividing the multi-syllable total by the overall word total, and multiplying the result by 100.

6.   Add this figure to your average sentence-length figure, and multiply the total by 0.4 (you can now see the reason for the calculator!)

Here's an example of the procedure:

1.	Length of passage (word count)	=	110
2.	Number of sentences	=	7
3.	Average sentence length (110 divided by 7)	=	16
4.	Number of words of 3+ syllables	=	12
5.	Percentage of multi-syllable words (12 divided by 110 multiplied by 100)	=	11
6.	Fog Index (11 + 16 = 27 multiplied by 0.4)	=	10.8

An Index of 10.8 would qualify as about average: clear, understandable, but capable of improvement. Now let us apply the Fog Index to some examples of published writing.

A leading article in the *Sun* newspaper:

> *A fortnight today Britain's future in Europe will be decided. / Not by the voters of Britain, / but by the voters of France. / Our Government has made it clear that if the French say 'Non' in their referendum, the Maastricht Treaty is dead. / If they say 'Oui', we can all go happily forward/ with no regard to how the British people may feel. / This is unacceptable. / Our people have never had the chance to vote on European unity. / Maastricht was not an Election issue / so it is quite arguable that Britain should have a referendum. / Mr Major believes that this kind of poll is 'undemocratic'. / Surely it can't be wrong if the ordinary man and woman – as well as MPs — have their say. /*

Total words: **122** Over two syllables: **9** Percentage: **9** Total sentences: **12** Average sentence length: **10**
Add **10** + **9** = **19**. Multiply by **0.4**.
Fog Index: **7.6** = sparklingly clear

From a *Sunday Telegraph* editorial on the same topic:

The spectacle of the French being allowed their say, / while the British people are silenced, / grows daily more intolerable. / We seldom have anything to learn about democracy from the land of Robespierre and Bonaparte, / but we do now. / On September 20 French voters will have the chance to give their verdict on the Maastricht Treaty, / and our own Government has said it will be bound by their decision. / The leaders of both main parties have conspired to suppress debate about Europe, / which they know would expose deep divisions among their followers. / They prevented Europe from becoming an issue in our general election / by the simple expedient of agreeing with each other. / The voter wishing to register his or her opposition to Maastricht was given no serious party for which to vote. / Our politicians have thereby spared themselves the disagreeable task of justifying their European policy to the public. /

Total words: **149** Over two syllables: **16** Percentage: **10**
Total sentences: **13** Average sentence length: **11.5**
Add **11.5 + 10 = 21.5**. Multiply by **0.4**
Fog Index: **8.6**. Despite the more elaborate construction, hardly less clear than the deliberately simplified tabloid Sun.

From *The Second World War: Triumph and Tragedy*, by Winston Churchill:

The final destruction of the German Army has been related; / it remains to describe the end of Hitler's other fighting forces./ During the previous autumn the German Air Force, / by a considerable feat of organisation, / but at the cost of its long-range bomber output, / had greatly increased the number of its fighter aircraft. / Our strategic bombing had thrown it on to the defensive / and 70 per cent of its fighters had to be used for home defence./ Although greater in numbers their effectiveness was less, / largely owing to fuel shortage caused by our attacks on oil installations, / which it became their principal duty to prevent. / German high-performance jet fighters perturbed us for a time, / but special raids on their centres of production and their airfields averted the threat. / Throughout January and February our bombers continued to attack, / and we made a heavy raid in the latter month on Dresden, then a centre of communications of Germany's Eastern Front. / The enemy air was fading. / As our troops advanced the airfields of the Luftwaffe were more and more squeezed into a diminishing area, / and provided excellent targets. /

Total words: **186** Over two syllables: **13** Percentage : **7**
Total sentences : **18** Average sentence length: **10**
Add **10 + 7 = 17**. Multiple by **0.4**

Fog Index: **6.8** Churchill, widely regarded as a master of English prose, remains an example to us all. Despite the awesome scale and complexity of what Churchill is describing, the average ten-year old could fully appreciate and comprehend this typical passage.

From *A Good Enough Parent: the guide to bringing up your child* by Bruno Bettelheim

> *Psychoanalytic doctrine is deeply committed to the conviction that how these inherited characteristics will be shaped depends on a person's life experiences./ Thus it subscribes to a historical view, / according to which later events are to a considerable degree conditioned by what has happened before; / therefore, the earliest history of the individual is of greatest importance in respect to what he will be like in his later life, / not only because it is the basis for all that follows but also because early history largely determines how later life will be experienced. / While genetic and evolutionary history creates an individual's potentialities, / his early personal history more than anything that follows accounts for the forms these potentialities will take in the actuality of his life.*

Total words: **125** Over two syllables: **20** Percentage: **16**
Total sentences: **7** Average sentence length: **18**
Add **18 + 16 = 34**. Multiply by **0.4**.
Fog Index: **13.6** An explanatory passage with a Fog Index this high is inappropriate for its intended audience. It's not the kind of writing to struggle with if you're looking for practical advice to help you bring up a child!

As dense as it is the passage above is relatively lucid when compared with one of our early examples of officialese:

> *A person shall be treated as suffering from physical disablement such that he is either unable to walk or virtually unable to do so if he is not unable or virtually unable to walk with a prosthesis or an artificial aid which he habitually wears or uses or if he would not be unable or virtually unable to walk if he habitually wore or used a prosthesis or an artificial aid which is suitable in his case. /*

Total words: **78** Over two syllables: **19** Percentage: **24**
Total sentences: **1** (the sheer overall obscurity prevents splitting this piece into subsentences) Average sentence length: **78**
Add **78 + 24 = 102**. Multiply by **0.4**
Fog Index: **40.8** A sure sign of impenetrable prose with a visibility factor of nil. Someone was unable, or virtually unable, to write plain English, prosthesis or no prosthesis.

Finally . . . testing the experts's expert: a passage from Fowler's *Modern English Usage*:

> *The use of semi-colons to separate parallel expressions that would normally be separated by commas is not in itself illegitimate, / but it*

must not be done when the expressions so separated form a group that is itself separated by nothing more than a comma, if that, from another part of the sentence. / To do this is to make the less include the greater, which is absurd . . . / As long as the Prayer-Book version of the Psalms continues to be read, the colon is not likely to pass quite out of use as a stop, / chiefly as one preferred to the semi-colon by individuals, or in impressive contexts, or in gnomic contrasts (Man proposes: God disposes); / but the time when it was second member of the hierarchy, full stop, colon, semi-colon, comma, is past. /

Total words: **133** Over two syllables: **12** Percentage: **9**
Total sentences: **6** Average sentence length: **22**
Add **9 + 22 = 31**. Multiply by **0.4**

Fog Index: **12.4** According to Robert Gunning's test, just the right side of the fog bank. You'd expect an extract from the grammarian's bible to do better; it was, after all, written by that master of correct language, H W Fowler. In fact it was taken from the edition of Fowler's *Modern English Usage* revised by the apostle of plain English, Sir Ernest Gowers (but, in fairness, dropped from the third, latest version edited by R W Burchfield).

There is another test by which that excerpt would receive a worse score for unreadability – one that we would heartily endorse. It's the Commonsense Test.

MAKING WORDS WORK FOR YOU: A refresher course in Grammar and Punctuation

Punctuation needn't be a pain: Stops, Commas and Other Marks

Sentences start with a Capital letter,
So as to make your writing better.
Use a full stop to mark the end –
It closes every sentence penned.

Victorian schoolmistress's Rules of Punctuation

Punctuation is the clear presentation of the written language. Or as *The Times* advises its journalists, it is 'a courtesy designed to help readers to understand a story without stumbling'.

It may help you to know something about its past. Two centuries ago most punctuation took its cues from speech. This was a period when the predominant practice of reading aloud, with its pauses and dramatic stresses, was translated into written punctuation – rhetorical punctuation.

A hundred years on, with increased literacy, the spoken word gave way to the written. The stress now was on meaning rather than dramatic effect, and rhetorical (or oratorical) punctuation bowed to a more logical system.

Today we have a blend of both: a system capable of conveying force, intonation, urgency, tension, rhythm and passion while never abandoning its duty to consistency and clarity of meaning.

Punctuation probably reached its zenith in the late 19th century, helping to make sense of fashionably-long sentences. The rules were fairly rigid, too. Now, the grammatical rules are more relaxed. Sentences, heavily influenced by the brevity of much newspaper usage, are shorter; the need for the complicated division of long sentences has disappeared. Commas are freely dropped where the meaning remains unaffected. The full stops after an abbreviation are disappearing in a general quest for typographic neatness.

81

Most people using the English language probably go through life without ever putting on paper any punctuation marks other than the comma, dash and full stop.

But while that may do for the majority it will be of little use to anyone who wants to be a better-than-average writer. The role of punctuation in writing good English cannot be underestimated. If your knowledge of this art is full of holes, or a bit rusty, here's a brief refresher course that should help banish confusion with capitals, hassles with hyphens and catastrophes with apostrophes.

Units of Space: sentences and paragraphs

Space is a basic form of punctuation. It separates words, sentences, paragraphs and larger units of writing such as chapters.

The sentence is about the most common of all grammatical units. We speak in sentences, and the most untutored letter-writers among us will use them while ignoring every other form of punctuation.

So what is a sentence? A sentence should express a single idea, complete in thought and construction. Like this:

The rare great crested newt was once called the great warty newt.

The sentence can be quite elastic, and punctuation allows us to expand it:

The rare great crested newt, which is native to Britain and rarely exceeds fifteen centimetres in length, was once called the great warty newt.

You'll notice how the cunning commas have allowed us to double the length of the sentence, adding fresh information without losing any of its original clarity. But sentences can also shrink, sometimes alarmingly:

Don't!

That single word, provided it is given meaning by other words or thoughts surrounding it, is a sentence, or, more correctly, a sentence fragment:

I went over to the door and tried to open it.
Don't!
I spun around, searching for the owner of the angry voice. In the darkness, a face appeared . . .

You can see here that not only the surrounding words, but also a range of spaces and punctuation marks, help to give that single word the meaning intended.

A question that crops up with worrying regularity is, 'How long should a sentence be?' The pat answer is, neither too long nor too short. Short sentences are easier to take but an endless succession of staccato sentences can irritate the reader. Conscientious writers will read their work aloud or mentally aloud as they proceed; that way the sentences are likely to form themselves into a logical, interesting, economical and, with luck, elegant flow of thought.

Probably the best definition of a paragraph is that of Sir Ernest Gowers: 'a unit of thought, not of length . . . homogenous in subject matter and sequential in treatment of it.' Perhaps, but of all the units of punctuation the paragraph is the least precise and the most resistant to rules. Sometimes they are indented, sometimes not. Sometimes they consist of a single line or a single word or leviathan examples that ramble on for a page or more.

Here are some useful pointers. Think of the end of a paragraph as a sort of breathing space for both speaker and listener. The speaker has reached a point of fresh departure, and the listener needs a brief break from concentration. In writing, a new paragraph marks a break or change in the flow of thought, which is as good a reason as any to begin on a fresh line.

Capital Letters

Capital letters are a form of punctuation in that they help to guide the eye and mind through a text. Try reading this:

> *on sunday, april 7, easter day, after having been at st paul's cathedral, i*
> *came to dr johnson, according to my usual custom. johnson and i supt at*
> *the crown and anchor tavern, in company with sir joshua reynolds, mr*
> *langton, mr [william] nairne, now one of the scotch judges, with the title*
> *of lord dunsinan, and my very worthy friend, sir william forbes, of pitsligo.*

That is a paragraph shorn of capital letters. It's readable, with some effort, but how much easier would the eye glide through it were it guide-posted with capitals at the start of each sentence, name and the abbreviation *Mr*!

Using capital letters to start sentences and surnames is clear enough, but a good deal of mystery surrounds the use of capitals in some other areas of writing. Here, then, is a brief guide:

Armed Forces	*British Army, Italian Navy, Brazilian Air Force,* but *army, navy, air force.* Ranks are capitalised: *Sergeant, Admiral, Lieutenant* etc.
The Calendar	*Monday, March, Good Friday, St Patrick's Day*
The Deity	*God, Father, Almighty. Holy Ghost, Jesus Christ;* also *Bible, New Testament, Koran, Talmud* etc; and religions (*Judaism, Baptists*).
Diplomatic	*Nicaraguan embassy* (*embassy* is lower-case)
Dog Breeds	*Labrador, Afghan hound, Scotch terrier* etc, but *rottweiler, lurcher, bulldog,* etc lower-case (check dictionary as capitalisation is inconsistent).
Exclamations	*Oh! Ahrrgh! Wow!*
First Person Pronoun	*I told them that I was going out.*

Flora and Fauna	*Arab horse, Shetland pony, Montague's harrier* but *hen harrier* (caps where a person's name is involved). Plants are lower-case but with scientific names, the first name, the genus, is capitalised: *Agaricus bisporus.*
Geographical	*The West, the East, the Orient, Northern Hemisphere, New World, British Commonwealth*
Heavenly Bodies	*Mars, Venus, Uranus, Ursa Major, Halley's Comet*
History and Historical Names	*Cambrian Era, Middle Ages, Elizabethan*
Local Government	*council*, but *Kent County Council, Lord Mayor of Manchester*
Member of Parliament	lower case except when abbreviated: *MP*
Personification	*The family gods were Hope and Charity*
The Pope	*pope*, but *Pope Paul, Pope John*, etc
Proper names	Names of people (*Tony Blair, Spice Girls*); places (*Europe, Mt Everest*); titles (*Pride and Prejudice, Nine O'Clock News*); epithets (*Iron Duke, Iron Lady*); nicknames (*'Tubby' Isaacs, 'Leadfoot' Evans*); races of people (*Aztecs, Shawnees*); nationalities (*Brits, Estonians*).
Religion	*Rev Adam Black, Fr O'Brien, Sister Wendy, Mother Teresa, Archbishop of Canterbury.*
Royalty	*The Queen, Duke of Edinburgh, Princess Anne*
Our Rulers	*Chancellor of the Exchequer, Secretary of State, House of Commons, Labour party* (note the small *p*)
Satirised References	*In Crowd, Heavy Brigade, She Who Must Be Obeyed*
Scouts	*Scouts, Guides, Cubs*
Seasons	*spring, summer, autumn, winter: all lower-case*
Trade names, marks	*Hoover, Peugeot, Kentucky Fried Chicken*
Titles	*Sir Thomas More, Lord Asquith, Mr and Mrs*
Van	When writing Dutch names *van* is lower-case when part of the full name (*Vincent van Gogh*) but capitalised when used only with the surname (*Van Gogh*)
von	In Germanic names, *von* is always lower-case
World War	Capitalise, as in *World War 1, World War 2.* The usage *first world war* or *second world war* is often preferred.

Devices for Separating and Joining The Full Stop

We now shrink from the paragraph to a minuscule dot: the **full stop**, full point or period. Minuscule it may be but, like atoms and germs, it packs a potent power. The full stop is the most emphatic, abrupt and unambiguous of all the punctuation marks.

Here's a passage displaying a variety of punctuation marks; the full stop, however, is easily the most predominant:

> *With intense frustration, Giles grabbed the man, surprising him.*
> *'No you don't!' he yelled hoarsely.*
> *The man recovered, fighting back. Fiercely. Savagely.*
> *Hard breathing. The wincing thud of fists. An alrming stream of*
> *crimson from Giles's left eye.*
> *Pulses racing, they glared at one another, each daring the other to make*
> *the next move. A car horn in the distance. Some shouts.*

That's stylised prose, and could be criticised for its over-use of sentence fragments rather than complete sentences. But here the heavy-handed application of the full stop is deliberate, for we can see what the writer is getting at – the harsh punch, punch, punch effect of a fist-fight.

At the other extreme many writers try to project a stream-of-consciousness effect by chucking out all punctuation, including full stops. One famous example is a passage in James Joyce's *Ulysses* which goes on and on for over a thousand words without so much as a pause. But he did need a full stop at the end!

Full stops control the length of your sentences, so remember:

- **Try to keep sentences variable in length, but generally short.**

- **Using long sentences doesn't necessarily make you a better writer.**

- **To use only full stops is as unnatural as walking without bending your legs. Consider the use of other punctuation marks.**

The Comma

The **comma** is the most flexible and most versatile of all the punctuation marks. And because it is also the least emphatic mark it is also the most complex and subtle. Not surprisingly, many writers feel a nagging uncertainty about using commas.

Perhaps the most resilient myth about commas is that they indicate breath pauses. There was some truth in this when the language was more orally inclined, but today commas have all but succumbed to grammatical logic.

> *Every winter, over fifty rare migratory species take advantage of the mild*
> *Norfolk climate.*

You can hear the lecturer intoning this, can't you – with a dramatic pause before announcing 'over fifty rare migratory species'. Try it. But when you write it as a sentence you soon find that the comma is redundant:

> *Every winter over fifty rare migratory species take advantage of the mild Norfolk climate.*

Most writing today requires commas that serve a logical purpose, but if you are a novelist, reporting a character's speech, you would be correct in using what are called 'rhetorical commas' when the character takes a natural breath.

Using commas effectively to make your writing more readable is a bit of a balancing act that requres thought and practice. Some writers over-use commas:

> *It is, curiously, surprising when, say, you hear your name announced in a foreign language, or even in a strange accent.*

Although grammatically correct that sentence seems to be hedged with *ifs*, *buts*, *maybes* and pontifications. Can it be rewritten without losing the meaning?

> *Curiously, it is surprising when, for example, you hear your name announced in a foreign language or even in a strange accent.*

The sentence, less two commas, is now a little more direct. Here's another sample, which can be rewritten without using any commas at all:

> *He had not, previously, met the plaintiff, except when, in 1974, he had, unexpectedly, found himself in Paris.*

Let's look a little closer at comma-reduction by taking a simple sentence:

A   *My hobby, train-spotting, is, to many, a bit of a joke.*
B   *My hobby, train-spotting, is to many, a bit of a joke.*
C   *My hobby, train-spotting, is to many a bit of a joke.*
D   *My hobby train-spotting is to many, a bit of a joke.*
E   *My hobby train-spotting is to many a bit of a joke.*

Pedants might claim that all these sentences differ in shades of meaning, but to the average reader they all mean the same thing. So we are left with choosing which one we would use to get our point across clearly and economically. Which version would you choose? (our choice would be **C**, but it is our personal preference and not one we would impose upon others.)

You are now probably aware that the ability to recognise where commas are needed is an acquired skill – but one worth pursuing. Merely scanning a sentence will usually tell you. The writer of the following sentence was either afraid of commas or intent on speed of delivery:

> *The land is I believe owned by the City Council.*

Most of us would call for commas after *is* and *believe*, because the phrase *I believe* is really an important qualifier and needs to be highlighted from the main statement, *The land is owned by the City Council*, which, by itself, may not be true. A more serious case of the comma-less sentence occurs when the lack of commas leads to ambiguity, and even hilarity.

> *As the car slowly sank in the bog over the road the neighbours laughed uproariously.*

Only a comma after *bog* will rescue the meaning from this confusing sentence. But a better idea would be to rewrite it:

> *As the car slowly sank in the bog, the neighbours over the road laughed uproariously.*

As a general rule, where including a comma helps clarity, put it in. Where dropping one doesn't endanger understanding but helps the flow of a sentence, leave it out.

A very common error in writing is the 'comma splice' – the use of a comma in place of a linking word to unite two sentences in the mistaken belief that it will form a single sentence:

> *The house is large, it has five bedrooms.*

This is not a grammatical sentence, but there are several ways to make it one:

> *The house is large; it has five bedrooms.*
> *The house is large because it has five bedrooms.*
> *The house is large and has five bedrooms.*
> *The house is large, with five bedrooms.*

Despite the faulty construction of the offending sentence, at least the meaning is clear. That, however, can't be said of the following miscreants where commas, or lack of them, create ambiguity:

> *They were sick and tired of the seemingly endless journey.*
> *They were sick, and tired of the seemingly endless journey.*
>
> *The animal spun an arrow through its heart.*
> *The animal spun, an arrow through its heart.*

In each of these cases the strategic placement of a comma, or the lack of one, completely changes the meaning of the statement.

The Functions of the Comma

● **Setting apart names and persons:**
Are you going to meet him tomorrow, John?
That, ladies and gentlemen, is the situation.
Darling, don't you think you've gone too far?

● **Itemising words:**
Please place all towels, costumes, clothing and valuables in the lockers.

● **Itemising word groups:**
Please place any articles of clothing, swimming and sporting equipment, personal belongings, but not money and jewellery, in the lockers.

● **Enclosing additional thoughts or qualifications:**
The occasion was, on the whole, conducted with great dignity.
The class thought it was, arguably, one of his finest novels.

● **Setting apart interjections:**
Look, I've had enough!
Oh, have it your way, then!

● **Indicating pauses before direct speech:**
Jill turned abruptly and said, 'If that's the way you feel, then go home!'

● **Introducing questions:**
You will be going soon, won't you?
She is marrying James next month, isn't she?

● **Emphasising points of view:**
Naturally, I'll look after her.
Of course, she fully deserves the prize.

● **Setting off comparative or contrasting statements:**
The taller they are, the farther they fall.
The more he adored her, the less she cared.

● **Reinforcing statements:**
She's ill because she simply won't eat, that's why!
It'll come right in the end, I'm sure.

Using Commas with Adjectives

See if you can work out, in these two sentences, why one has the adjectives separated by commas, and the other does not:

The night resounded with a loud, chilling, persistent ringing.
It was a large brick Victorian mansion.

The reasons are embodied in two seemingly simple rules worth remembering:

- **Where the adjectives (or other modifiers) define separate attributes (*loud, chilling, persistent*), they are best separated by commas.**
- **Where the adjectives work together to create a single image (*large, brick, Victorian*), the commas are best avoided.**

Two seemingly simple rules, but they can be tricky to apply. Sometimes you may be led into ambiguity, and have to resort to commonsense:

Myra was a pretty smart young woman.
Myra was a pretty, smart young woman.

Well, does the writer mean that Myra was pretty and smart, or just very smart?

The Oxford, or Final Comma

The Times advises its journalists to 'avoid the so-called Oxford comma: *x, y and z* and not *x, y, and z*'. What this means is that:

Martin spoke to Edith, Lesley, Bunty and Samantha.

is preferred to

Martin spoke to Edith, Lesley, Bunty, and Samantha.

Quite good advice; a final comma before *and* in a list is now outmoded – unless there is the possibility of ambiguity:

The colours are red, blue and white.

Does this mean three separate colours, or two – red, and blue and white in some sort of combination? It's possible, so in this case a comma after *blue* might be wise to make sure that everyone gets the message that we're talking about three colours.

Other Problem Comma Placements

It has been customary to enclose adverbs and adverbial phrases (*however, indeed, for example, anyway, on the contrary,* etc) with commas:

You are, nevertheless, guilty of the first charge.

However the trend today is to dispense with such commas if the meaning of a statement is clear without them:

You are nevertheless guilty of the first charge.

But always read over such sentences carefully to avoid ambiguous clangers such as:

The hospital informed us that both victims were happily recovering.

When what was really meant was:

The hospital informed us that both victims were, happily recovering.

You'll also find that commas are needed for sentences beginning with adverbs, such as:

Curiously, the two scientists had never met.

Sometimes you will find that verbs will need enclosing by commas to help guide readers through a complex passage:

In the daytime, sleeping, the baby was adorable, but at nights, howling continuously, she was a tyrant and a monster.

One of the most common instances of misplacement occurs when a comma is inserted before an *and* when, logically, it should have been dropped in after:

WRONG: *He glanced at the clock, and abruptly closing his book, leapt up from the chair.*

RIGHT: *He glanced at the clock and, abruptly closing his book, leapt up from the chair.*

Using Commas as Parenthesis

One of the most interesting, but also perhaps the most contentious, use of commas, is to parenthesise (or bracket) relevant but not essential matter from the main part of a sentence:

The wild hyacinths (which are now at the height of their season) tint the woods with a pale blue mist.

The essential message here is *The wild hyacinths tint the woods with a pale blue mist*. But then we've had a further thought – *which are now at the height of their season* – which we'd like to include in the same sentence. Sometimes we enclose such additions in **parenthesis** (brackets) as above, but mostly we use a pair of far more convenient and less disruptive commas:

The wild hyacinths, which are now at the height of their season, tint the woods with a pale blue mist.

Now that we've seen how commas are used to isolate subordinate statements, what are these commas doing in this sentence:

The two lead actors, who appear in 'Grease', won their respective roles after a gruelling eight years in musicals.

The two enclosing commas here are telling us that *who appear in Grease* is non-essential information. But if you rewrite the sentence without that phrase it doesn't make sense: we don't know who the lead actors are or what they are doing. In fact 'who appear in Grease' is called a defining or restrictive phrase – one that identifies, modifies or qualifies its subject. So the sentence should read:

> *The two lead actors who appear in 'Grease' won their respective roles after a gruelling eight years in musicals.*

There is, as you can see, no choice in this matter, and to get it wrong will leave most readers floundering in a swamp of ambiguity and confusion.

This handy two-comma convention allows us to determine instantly what, in any sentence, is essential to the subject of the sentence and what is not. But always be on guard against misunderstanding:

> **A**   *Women from Liverpool, who can't swim, are likely to drown.*
> **B**   *Women from Liverpool who can't swim are likely to drown.*

In **A** the writer appears to be insulting the good women of Liverpool by suggesting that none of them can swim. In **B**, though, the phrase *who can't swim* defines just those women who could be in danger of drowning.

To summarise:

- **Where a phrase or clause does not define or qualify the subject, indicate that it is non-essential matter by isolating it with a pair of commas.**
- **Where a phrase or clause defines or qualifies the subject, weld it to the subject by omitting the commas.**

The Semicolon

Semicolons make some writers nervous but once you get the hang of them you'll find they are very useful punctuation marks. They have a number of grammar and style functions:

- **Using semicolons to join words, word groups and sentences**

Occasionally we find ourselves writing a long sentence with too many connecting words such as *and, but* and *also*, with the danger of getting into an impossible tangle:

> *The history of the semicolon and colon is one of confusion because there are no precise rules governing their use and, furthermore, many writers would argue that both marks are really stylistic rather than parenthetical, and that they can easily be replaced by commas, full stops and dashes, and there the argument rests.*

There's nothing grammatically wrong with that but it is unwieldy and unappealing to both eye and mind. Many writers would, without much hesitation, recast it as two or more separate sentences:

> *The history of the semicolon and colon is one of confusion. There are no*
> *precise rules governing their use. Many writers argue that both marks*
> *are really stylistic rather than parenthetical, and that they can easily be*
> *replaced by commas, full stops or dashes. And there the argument rests.*

We have previously seen how the judicious use of full stops to achieve shorter sentences can aid understanding, and that is certainly the case here. But some writers, feeling that the original long sentence is, after all, about a single subject and should therefore be kept as a whole and not split apart, would turn to the semicolon to achieve unity of thought without sacrificing clarity:

> *The history of the semicolon and colon is one of confusion; there are no*
> *precise rules governing their use; many writers argue that both marks*
> *are really stylistic rather than parenthetical and that they can easily be*
> *replaced by commas, full stops or dashes; and there the argument rests.*

● **Using semicolons to separate word groups containing commas**

Any sentence that is essentially a list should be crystal clear and easily read. Most 'sentence lists' adequately separate the items with commas, but sometimes the items themselves are groups containing commas and require semicolons for clarity. These two examples demonstrate how handy semicolons can be:

> *Those present included Mr and Mrs Allison, their daughters Sarah,*
> *Megan and Sue; the Smith twins; Reg and Paul Watson; Joyce, Helen*
> *and Bill Hobson; etc.*

● **Semicolons can restore order to a sentence suffering from 'Comma Riot'**

Here's a longish but reasonably accomplished sentence spoiled by 'comma riot':

> *His main aims in life, according to Wilma, were to achieve financial*
> *independence, to be powerfully attractive, not only to women but in*
> *particular to rich ladies, to eat and drink freely without putting on*
> *weight, to remain fit, vital and young-looking beyond his eightieth*
> *birthday and, last but not least, to not only read, but fully understand,*
> *Stephen Hawking's 'A Brief History of Time'.*

Many good writers would defend this sentence, despite its eleven commas. But others, perhaps more concerned with clarity than rhythm, would suggest that some of the thoughts at least should be separated by the longer pauses provided by semicolons:

> *His main aims in life, according to Wilma, were to achieve financial*
> *independence; to be powerfully attractive, not only to women but in*
> *particular to rich ladies; to eat and drink freely without putting on*
> *weight; to remain fit, vital and young-looking beyond his eightieth*
> *birthday and, last but not least, to not only read but fully understand*
> *Stephen Hawking's 'A Brief History of Time'.*

● **Using semicolons to provide pauses before certain adverbs**

There are certain adverbs and conjunctions that require a preceding pause, but one longer and stronger than that provided by a comma. Look at this example:

WITH A COMMA:	*It was a beautiful car, moreover it was*
	economical to run.
WITH A SEMICOLON:	*It was a beautiful car; moreover it was*
	economical to run.

You can see and hear that need for a pause before *moreover*, can't you?

A comma is wrong for both grammar and rhetoric. Here's another example; read it and note your instinctive pause before *nevertheless*:

> *Joe claimed he'd beaten the bookies on every race; nevertheless he was*
> *broke as usual when he left the track.*

Watch out for *therefore, however, besides, also, moreover, furthermore, hence, consequently* and *subsequently*; in many constructions they will require a preceding semicolon.

Trouble with your Colon?

Although under threat from the dash, the colon is a versatile workhorse, and many colon-doubters are stopped in their tracks when confronted with the range of its functions.

● **Using the colon to point the reader's attention forward**

In this role the colon acts as a pointing finger, as if to warn the reader about a statement ahead: 'Wait for it . . here it comes!' Or, in the more eloquent words of the grammarian Henry Fowler, its function is 'that of delivering the goods that have been invoiced in the preceding words'. The 'goods' might be a conclusion, a list, a summary or a contrasting statement:

> *Maddeningly beautiful, honey-voiced, overwhelmingly generous, owner*
> *of three luxury homes: Anna was an object of desire to any man.*

- **Using the colon to introduce a list**

  This is perhaps where colons are most commonly used:

  The hotel had everything: pool, sauna, Jacuzzi, gym, hairdresser, tanning booths and even a dietician.

- **Using the colon to present an explanation or example**

  The beleaguered bank closed its doors after just three days: not surprising when you saw the list of directors.

- **Using the colon to introduce direct speech**

  Although most stylists insist that commas are the correct marks to introduce direct speech, the use of colons today hardly earns a frown:

  The Mayor strode up to the platform, opened his notes and glared at the assembly: 'You have not come here tonight for nothing,' he growled.

- **Using the colon to present a conclusion**

  Fifty-three years in the business suggested to him there was only one certainty in life: the inevitability of change.

- **Using the colon as a substitute for a conjunction**

  In this example the writer preferred the punchier colon to a choice of conjunctions such as *and* or *but*:

  Rodriguez downed him with a dazzling left hook that came from nowhere: Hayman did not get up.

- **Using colons to introduce questions, quotations and subtitles**

QUESTION:	*The essential question is simply this: did she or did she not seduce Sir Timothy?*
QUOTATION:	*Rachel's thoughts were neatly summed up by Swift: 'That flattery's the food of fools; Yet now and then your men of wit will condescend to take a bit'.*
SUBTITLE:	*Gilbert White: Observer in God's Little Acre*

- **Using the colon to link contrasting statements**

  In this role the colon steps into the ring with the semi-colon, which also has the ability to administer a mild shock. The choice is a matter of taste:

  She cooks: I eat.
  Jeremy had only one small fault: he was an inveterate liar.

  It's worth remembering that:

● The difference between a colon and a semicolon is not a difference in weight or force; the two marks are mostly used for quite different purposes
● A colon is never followed by a capital letter, except with proper nouns: *Emma, Ford Motor Co*, etc.

And also take note that the colon is widely misused, or used unnecessarily as in this example:

WRONG: *The man was amazing and was able to play: the piano, violin, double bass, trombone, clarinet, harp and drums.*

The Seductive Embrace of the Bracket

In our discussion of commas we saw how material could be set apart or parenthesised (the term parenthesis, via Latin and Greek, means 'an insertion besides') by placing it between two commas.

The sentence above is just such an example, except that instead of using a pair of commas we have used a pair of brackets or, more correctly, **parentheses** or **round brackets** ( ).

If you look at that first sentence again, you will see that the brackets serve to set apart relevant matter but which could, if you wished to be ruthless, be dropped altogether.

So what's the difference between commas and brackets? Generally, material within commas is still very much part of the sentence, and must observe the grammatical conventions of the sentence. Bracketed material, on the other hand, is more distanced from the main sentence. Brackets also release the writer from a lot of responsibility. The parenthesised material, leading a 'separate life', is not required grammatically to match the sentence into which it is inserted.

The bracket's embrace is seductive and extremely adaptable, as the following catalogue of examples of usage demonstrates:

ADDING INFORMATION	*One of the earliest dictionaries is that of Elisha Coles (London, 1685).*
EXPLANATION	*Unable to follow the French instructions and after nothing but trouble he returned the car (a Renault saloon) to the garage.*
AFTERTHOUGHT	*During the tour they visited at least a dozen cities and towns (but why not, we wondered, Paris and Marseilles?) in just ten days.*
CLARIFICATION	*The directive stated quite clearly (page 15, second paragraph) that the department would close from March 1.*

COMMENT	*The women of Brayville were refused admission (why?) earlier that day.*
ILLUSTRATION	*The candidate spent far too long discussing irrelevancies (20 minutes on the price of footwear; another ten on tax havens) with the inevitable result that we walked out.*
INDICATING OPTIONS	*Your document(s) will be returned in due course.*

The Square Bracket

Square brackets are not angular versions of parentheses; they have a different function entirely. Unlike matter within round brackets, words enclosed in square brackets are intended to be not part of a sentence, but an editorial or authorial insert:

> *It was a matter of opinion that if offered the position, he [Professor Brandmeyer] would most likely refuse it on moral grounds.*

That sentence came at the end of a very long paragraph. The professor's name had been mentioned at the beginning, but other names and a lot of discussion followed so that the late reference to he was in danger of being misunderstood. The editor therefore inserted the name [*Professor Brandmeyer*] in square brackets to remove any doubt and also to indicate that the intervention was the editor's and not the author's.

One of the most common uses of square brackets is to enclose the adverb *sic* (from the Latin *sicut*, meaning 'just as') to indicate that incorrect or doubtful matter is quoted exactly from the original:

> *Pink and yellow concubines [sic] climbed in great profusion up the trellis. Miss Patricia Wall Wall [sic] with her fiance Mr Gerald Kleeman.*

The latter example was a caption under a photograph of the newly engaged couple; *The Times* wanted to make sure that readers understood that 'Wall Wall' really was the young lady's surname and not a misprint.

A Dash to the rescue!

Although the dash is a mark much maligned – especially by punctuation purists who decry its use instead of the colon – it has in recent times attracted a growing band of defenders. 'It's the most exciting and dramatic punctuation mark of them all!' they claim.

Others admire the dash for its flexibility and disdain for rules. It is a bit of a larrikin and a lot of fun in the often po-faced world of punctuation.

Here are some of the respectable ways in which the dash will be found useful:

LINKING DEVICE	*Mrs Sims had four small daughters – Poppy, Iris, Pansy and Petal.*
AS A PAUSE	*Everyone expected the speaker to be controversial – but not to the extent of swearing.*
SIGNALLING SURPRISE OR PARADOX	*A straight line is the shortest distance between two points – when you're sober.*
	Then the adhesive gave way, the beard came adrift and Santa Claus was revealed as – Aunt Mildred!
INDICATING	*There will be, of course, er – a small charge, because –*
HESITATION	*well, er –*
SEPARATING LISTS	*She assembled all the ingredients – flour, sugar, eggs, and raisins – and started on the pudding.*
AFTERTHOUGHTS	*They babbled on, delighted at sighting the rare parakeet – I didn't see so much as a feather.*

If you use dashes to set apart (as in separating lists), remember to insert the second dash, and not a comma or semicolon.

Quotation Marks

Quotation marks or 'inverted commas'? If you look at a newspaper or book and examine these marks closely you'll see that only the opening mark is inverted – that is, with the 'tail of the tadpole' pointing up; the closing mark is a normal raised or hanging comma or pair of commas. So we should use the term **quotation marks** (or **quotes** for short) exclusively.

Another point about quotation marks is whether to use single ('single') marks or double ("double") marks:

> *Heather said flatly, 'I never want to see him again.'*
> *Heather said flatly, "I never want to see him again."*

Newspapers and book publishers are divided on this; some use single quotes, others double – it's a matter of taste. But whether you use single or double marks you need to be aware of the convention for enclosing a quote within a quote. If you pefer single quotes, a quote within a quote must use double quotes. And vice versa:

The sales assistant said, 'We only have them in grey and blue but yesterday my boss told me, "I don't know why they don't make them in other colours."'

On the very rare occasions where it is found necessary to have a third quote within a second quote in the same sentence, the formula is single/double/single, or double/single/double.

Quoting direct speech

When we read a newspaper report or story we want to know when we're reading reported or interpreted speech and when we're reading words actually spoken. Quotation marks help us to differentiate between the two forms:

> *Mr Murphy said that in his view the value of the pound would drop towards the end of the year. 'I also believe most European currencies will follow suit,' he added.*

This tells us that the writer has summarised the first part of the statement in his own words, and we have to accept that his summary is a correct version of what Mr Murphy said. But we should have no doubts about the accuracy of the second part of the statement because the quote marks have signalled that the words are exactly what he said. When you are quoting direct speech you must ensure that the words enclosed by your quotation marks are exactly those spoken. Not approximately, but exactly. Important legal actions have been won and lost on this point.

It is also vital to make sure your reader knows who is responsible for the quoted statement. This is usually accomplished with what is called a **reporting clause**, which can introduce the statement or follow it or even interrupt it:

1.　　*Jones stated, 'I am innocent and I can easily prove it.'*
2.　　*'I am innocent and I can easily prove it,' Jones stated.*
3.　　*'I am innocent,' Jones stated, 'and I can easily prove it.'*

Another point to remember is that when quoted speech is interrupted by a reporting clause, two rules apply. If the quoted statement is interrupted at the end of a sentence it should be finished with a comma and resumed with a capital letter:

> *'I knew I'd seen that bird before,' said Gavin. 'It was a cormorant, wasn't it?'*

But if the speech is interrupted mid-sentence, it should be resumed in lower-case:

> *'Don't you agree,' asked Gavin, 'that the bird over there is a cormorant?'*

How to close quotations

It is easy to remind writers not to forget to close their quotations. What is a little more difficult is . . . how? Look at this example:

> *He then asked her, 'Do you think I'm drunk'?*

Do you place the question mark outside the quotation mark that closes the direct speech, or inside?

> *He then asked her, 'Do you think I'm drunk?'*

The answer is that it depends on the relationship between the quotation and the sentence that contains it. The rule is – and pay attention, now! –

> PUNCTUATION MARKS (full stops, commas, question and exclamation marks, etc) GO **INSIDE** THE FINAL QUOTATION MARK IF THEY RELATE TO THE QUOTED WORDS BUT **OUTSIDE** IF THEY RELATE TO THE WHOLE SENTENCE.

In our example, the question mark relates only to the quoted statement, *Do you think I'm drunk?* and so it rightly belongs inside the final quote mark. But let's change the sentence slightly:

> *Should he have asked her, 'Do you think I'm drunk'?*

You can see that now the question is an essential part of the whole sentence. To be pedantic about it, the sentence should properly be written like this:

> *Should he have asked her, 'Do you think I'm drunk?'?*

Here you see that the quotation has its own question mark inside the final quote mark (quite correctly), and the overall sentence has its mark outside (again correctly). But the two question marks look silly and everyone accepts that in a case like this the inside question mark can be dropped without causing confusion.

Most punctuation marks are multi-functional and quotation marks are no exception. They can be used to indicate titles (*His favourite film was the Marx Brothers' classic, 'Duck Soup'*); to identify nicknames (*Henry 'Rabbit Punch' Watson; Al 'Scarface' Capone*); to indicate doubt, cynicism or disbelief (*the hamburgers contained a mixture of liver, chicken parts and 'beef'*); and to indicate that a word or phrase should not be taken literally (*We are 'giving away' this nationally advertised Pyramid X100 Fresh Air Ioniser for only £17.95*).

Hassles with Hyphens

The hyphen helps us construct words to help clarify meaning. At least that's what they set out to do. Take these two similar newspaper headlines:

> *MAN EATING TIGER SEEN NEAR MOTORWAY*
> *MAN-EATING TIGER SEEN NEAR MOTORWAY*

The first headline suggests that a hungry gourmet has decided to barbecue some choice jungle beast near a motorway, while the second could prove fatal should you be carelessly wandering along the hard shoulder. A hyphen has made all the difference.

In the same vein, *a little used car* (say a Mini) is not the same as a *little-used car* (say a block-long Roller with only 3,000 miles on the clock). Nor is a *small businessman* a *small-businessman*, or a *French polisher* a *French-polisher*.

Hyphens are used to join two or more associated words. Sometimes the marriage is permanent. A *book seller* became a *book-seller* but is now a *bookseller*; *life like* got engaged as *life-like* and is now well and truly married as *lifelike*. Many other common words began their careers as two words linked by a hyphen: *anticlimax, earring, lampshade, postgraduate, prehistoric, seaside, today, washbowl.*

Then there are hyphenated couples never destined to become permanent partners because of 'letter collision' which is visually confusing: *shell-like* (not *shelllike*); *semi-illiterate* (not *semiilliterate*); *de-ice* (not *deice*) – although we accept such unhyphenated words as *cooperative* and *coordination.*

Generally, hyphens are usual after the prefixes *ex-* (*ex-cop*); *non-* (*non-starter*) and *self-* (*self-employed*). They are not usually required after *anti-* (*antifreeze*); *counter-* (*counterweight*); *co-* (*coreligionist*); *neo-* (*neoclassicism*); *pre-* (*prehensile*) and *un-*(*unconditional*). But there are exceptions: *co-respondent* (*to distinguish it from a misspelt correspondent!*) and *re-creation* (*not recreation*).

A Hotch-potch of Hyphens

Here's a handy list of words and names that are usually, but not always, hyphenated:

anti-abortion
bone-shaking, bull's-eye, brother-in-law
call-up, cat-o'-nine-tails, Coca-Cola, co-worker
daddy-longlegs, daughter-in-law, deaf-and-dumb; deep-sea fishing, do-it-yourself, double-cross, double-dealing, double-park, Dow-Jones
ear-splitting, ex-husband, ex-serviceman
face-saving, foot-and-mouth disease, forget-me-not, four-letter-word, fractions *(three-quarters)*
get-together, give-and-take, good-for-nothing, good-looking
habit-forming, half-and-half, half-breed (almost all words prefixed with *half-* carry a hyphen), *helter-skelter, higgledy-piggledy, high-spirited, high-tech, hit-and-run*
ill-advised, ill-timed, ill-treat, infra-red
jack-o'-lantern, jiggery-pokery, Johnny-come-lately
knock-for-knock, Ku-Klux-Klan
lady-in-waiting, large-scale, Land-Rover, Latter-day Saint, left-handed, light-headed, lily-white, long-distance runner/telephone call, loose-limbed, low-key
man-of-war, middle-aged, mother-in-law, mother-of-pearl, muu-muu
near-sighted, ne'er-do-well, non-starter
O-level, off-peak, off-putting, old-fashioned, one-night-stand, out-of-doors
passer-by, penny-pinching, place-name, point-to-point, post-natal, pre-natal, price-fixing, pro-Irish, pro-life, etc
quick-tempered, quick-witted
right-handed, right-minded, rye-grass
St Martin-in-the-Fields, Saint-Saens, sawn-off, set-aside, short-change, son-in-law
test-tube baby, three-ring circus, tie-break, tip-off, T-shirt, trap-door spider, tutti-frutti,

tut-tut
*u*ltra-violet (but just as often *ultraviolet*)
vice-presidential
walk-on, walk-in, walkie-talkie, weather-beaten, weather-bound, well-known
X-chromosone, X-ray (or *x-ray*)
Y-chromosome, yo-heave-ho, yo-ho-ho

Symbols of Meaning
Questions and Exclamations

So far we've dealt with units of **space**, **separation** and **connection**. The rest of our punctuation marks are units or symbols of **expression** and **meaning**.

The **question mark** and **exclamation** mark share a common ancestry. The question mark has the squiggle atop the stop , not unlike a 'q' (for query?), while the exclamation mark consists of a hanging stroke pointing emphatically to the stop to make the reader screech to a halt.

The Question Mark

A sentence that asks a question requires a question mark, but a sentence that poses an indirect question does not:

DIRECT QUESTION   *'Are you going to the match?'*
INDIRECT QUESTION   *I asked him if he was going to the match.*

This looks pretty simple but sometimes an indirect question can be disguised:

A hundred years after Freud, fifty after the development of potent psychiatric drugs, have our ideas of psychiatric care really progressed, asks Dr Anthony Clare.

Not a question mark in sight. Why? Another headline, from *The Times*:

Why should allegations that go unchallenged in America be the subject of legal action in Britain, asks Roy Greenslade.

Both sentences seem to be shouting for question marks – in the the first after *progressed*, in the second after *Britain*. But if you look closer you will see that both sentences are novel forms of the indirect question. The second example might be rewritten as:

Roy Greenslade asks why should allegations that go unchallenged in America be the subject of legal action in Britain.

The 'Semi'-question

One use of the direct question is in the form of a polite request:

Would you let me know if either Monday or Tuesday next week is suitable?

There's little doubt there that a question mark is required. But here's another similar request-question:

Would you be good enough to ensure that in future cars and other vehicles belonging to non-staff are parked outside the gates.

Well, what is it – a request or a question? It is in fact part question, part-demand, and writer and reader both sense that a question mark would tend to weaken its authority. Many writers are troubled by this weasel-like quality. Look at these examples – all questions – and all quite comfortable without a question mark:

You're not going to give in yet, I trust.
I hope you're not calling me a liar.
I wonder if I might borrow the car tomorrow.

In these cases, the expressions of personal feeling – *I trust, I hope* and *I wonder* – tend to undermine the question content of the sentence. If you wrote *You're not going to give in yet?* you'd unhesitatingly finish with a question mark. But there are some questions that look quite strange with a question mark:

How dare you?　　　*How dare you!*

Here the expression is more an angry exclamation than a query, and a question mark would, in most cases, seem inappropriate.

The Exclamation Mark

Discouraged, if not banned, by many modern newspapers (where it is referred to as a 'startler', 'gasper', 'screamer' and by tabloid sub-editors as a 'dog's dick'), and with a reputation for over-use, the exclamation mark nevertheless earns its keep with a surprisingly wide range of uses.

It's hard to imagine the following examples carrying anything like the same force and feeling without the screamers:

Shut up!　You bitch!　What a mess!　Damn!

Literature would undoubtedly be the poorer without them. Good writers aren't afraid of exclamation marks and use them judiciously for a number of functions:

CONVEYING ANGER	*You're out of your mind!*
SCORN, DISGUST	*You must be joking!*

INDICATING IRONY AND **REVERSE MEANING**	*Thanks a lot!* *That's lovely, that is!*
UNDERLINING INSULTS **AND EXPLETIVES**	*You bastard!* *Shit!*
CONVEYING **IRONIC TONE**	*You're not so smart!* *And you thought we wouldn't win!*
COMMANDING	*Come here! Right now! Get lost!*

Catastrophes with Apostrophes

Most of us have seen and chortled over everyday apostrophic clangers like these:

> *Lilie's, Anemone's and Mum's* (London Florist)
> *Fresh Asparagu's* (Edinburgh greengrocer)
> *Her's is a warm, informal home* (newspaper interview)
> *Bargain Mens Shirt's* (street market sign)
> *This school and it's playground will be closed over Easter* (sign on gate at a Croydon school)

If we're honest most of us have to admit that there are times when we are forced to think quite hard about the use – or non-use – of apostrophes. So what's the problem?

The problem should disappear the moment we accept that there are only two kinds of apostrophes. One kind indicates the possession of something; the other kind indicates a contraction – a letter or letters left out of a word:

| **POSSESSIVE**
APOSTROPHE | *Did you know Jack's car is a write-off?*
I heard that Jack's kids have the flu. |
| **CONTRACTION**
APOSTROPHE | *Did you know that Jack's had a bad accident?*
I heard that Jack's in hospital. |

In the first two examples the apostrophe tells us that the car and the kids belong to Jack; that is a **possessive apostrophe**. In the second pair of examples the apostrophe tells us that something is left out: that *Jack's* is a shortened version of two or more words: that is a **contraction apostrophe**. We are expected to work out what these are and with experience we soon learn to fill in the gaps. In these cases *Jack's* is short for *Jack has* and *Jack is*.

Possessive Apostrophes

If we wish to indicate that something is possessed by somebody we use the possessive apostrophe:

Joyce's house, Bill's lawnmower, a boy's bike, his uncle's car

Possession, ownership or association can also apply to things:

a good day's work, the company's policy, the tree's branches

And the same goes for certain plural nouns:

men's trousers, children's toys, mice's tails, people's charter

No problems there. But all the above examples have something in common: none of the possessor words or names end with an *s* – *Joyce, Bill, boy, uncle, day, tree, men, people*, etc. So what's the big deal about words ending with an *s*?

The big deal is that adding possessive apostrophes to words and names such as *boss, surplus, Thomas*, and to plurals such as *cats, hours* and *friends*, is not such a straightforward business. Let's check some examples:

SINGULAR WORDS AND NAMES ENDING WITH 'S'	POSSESSIVE FORM
the boss	*the boss's temper*
Thomas	*Thomas's recent illness*
mistress	*a mistress's secrets*
Charles Dickens	*Dickens's novels*

Now look at what happens with plural nouns that end with 's':

PLURAL WORDS ENDING WITH 'S'	POSSESSIVE FORM
Penny's parents	*Penny's parents' caravan*
her friends	*her friends' parties*
the members	*the members' privileges*
our employees	*our employees' bonuses*
the girls	*the girls' classroom*

Get the picture? For singular ownership we simply add '*s*, but for plural or shared ownership we add the apostrophe after the *s* – *s*'. The system enables us to distinguish the different meanings. When we read,

The opera star heard the girl's singing

we understand that only one girl is singing, whereas

The opera star heard the girls' singing

tells us (if we've learnt the rules!) that the diva is listening to many girls singing. In some cases we have some free choices, according to taste. We can add the final '*s* (*Tom Jones's songs; Prince Charles's opinions*) or drop it

(*Wales' ruggedness; Dickens' characters; Jesus' teachings*), or observe tradition (*Queens' College, Cambridge; Queen's College, Oxford*).

However, beware of adjectives that look like possessives such as *games mistress* which require no apostrophe. And watch our for units of time, such as *a day's work, a minute's delay* and *six month's salary* in complex sentences such as these:

> *I'm taking three weeks holiday in three weeks' time.*
> *An hour's delay or two hours' delay – I wish the airline would make up its mind!*

Pronouns can be perplexing, too. Some have apostrophes and some do not:

PRONOUNS WITH APOSTROPHES	*one's problems, anyone's idea, someone's shoes, one another's responsibilities, nobody's fault, anybody's luggage, each other's possessions*
PRONOUNS WITHOUT APOSTROPHES	*his, hers, its, ours, yours, theirs*

Contraction Apostrophes

One of the most frequent errors is the use of *it's* for the possessive form of *it*. This is wrong, of course: *it's* is the accepted contraction for *it is* or *it has*. For the record, once and for all:

POSSESSION	*The newspaper claimed **its** punctuation record was unmatched by any of **its** rivals.*
CONTRACTION	***It's** (It is) a fact that the punctuation record of the newspaper **isn't** (is not) so clever after all.*

Also for the record is this list of most of the accepted contractions:

aren't	*are not*	*she'll*	*she will, she shall*
can't	*cannot, can not*	*she's*	*she is, she has*
couldn't	*could not*	*there's*	*there is*
hasn't	*has not*	*they'll*	*they will, they shall*
haven't	*have not*	*they're*	*they are*
he'll	*he will, he shall*	*they've*	*they have*
he's	*he is, he has*	*we'll*	*we will, we shall*
I'd	*I would, I had*	*weren't*	*were not*
I'll	*I will, I shall*	*we've*	*we have*
I'm	*I am*	*who's*	*who is, who has*
it's	*it is, it has*	*won't*	*will not*
I've	*I have*	*wouldn't*	*would not*
let's	*let us*	*you'll*	*you will, you shall*
ma'am	*madam*	*you're*	*you are*
mustn't	*must not*	*you've*	*you have*

There are a lot more everyday but irregular contractions: *sweet'n'low, 'alf a mo', finger lickin'* , *Ah'm talkin' to yuh*, and so forth; and an increasing number of businesses and institutions that have dropped their apostrophes: *Lloyds Bank, Gas Consumers Council, Missing Persons Bureau, Pears Soap*.

One final apostrophic tip: *who's* is short for *who is* or *who has*; *whose* indicates possession.

Punctuation Pot-pourri

We now come to the litter of punctuation . . . a few dots here, a stroke there, stars and bullets . . . and all of them can be put to work on occasional odd jobs.

The Three-dot Ellipsis

The science fiction pioneer H G Wells is credited with the invention of this mark . . . the **three-dot ellipsis**. In fact, Mrs Henry Wood was known to use the mark at least a couple of decades earlier, in the immortal line, 'Dead! and . . . never called me mother.' What this line of dots does is indicate missing matter, more or less saying, 'well, it's over to you, reader . . . '

The omitted matter may be a single word:

'Get the . . . out of here!'

or matter considered to be non-essential:

Yesterday the shares stood at just over £4.60 which if you believe last night's closing statement . . . at that price the company is valued at almost £1.6 billion.

or an implied quotation or phrase which the reader is expected to know:

So then she bought contact lenses . . . you know, men don't make passes . . . and she really believes that, too!

or indicating an unfinished thought:

The troubling question was, would Mrs Benedict sue, or . . .

or, indicating a time lapse:

Kimball crashed to the floor with eye-wincing force . . . only later, much later, in the darkness, did he realise he was a marked man.

or, indicating disjointed speech:

She paced the room. 'I don't know . . . every way I look at it . . . what would you do?' She drew deeply on the cigarette. 'I mean, surely he wouldn't do this to me . . . or would he?'

Asterisks

This complaining letter to *The Times* adequately explains one role of the asterisk:

> *In your paper last week I noticed a f***, a b***** and a f***ing and*
> *this made me wonder just who you think comprises your readership. If*
> *you feel that you have to censor any word that could possibly upset*
> *anybody, why do we not have M****** He***tine, the M********t*
> *Treaty and the C***** Ag********** P****y?**

The final asterisk is in its customary role of guiding the reader to a footnote or explanation elsewhere in the text, thus:

> **Michael Heseltine, Maastricht Treaty, Common Agricultural Policy*

Bullets

In our busy age the **bullet point (●)** has found increasing favour, perhaps because:

- It is the quickest way to summarise a series of facts or conclusions;
- It signals to the eye that here are the essentials;
- It encourages writers to be brief: using words and phrases rather than sentences;
- It captures readers who are too lazy or too harassed to read solid texts.

The stroke

Fancily called the virgule, solidus, shilling mark, slash and diagonal, the oblique **stroke** has a few limited uses:

TO INDICATE OPTIONS	*It depends upon how he/she behaves.*
	The situation calls for guile and/or force.
TO SEPARATE LINES	*The mist as it rises / touched with gold of*
OF VERSE	*the morning / Veils over the sadness / and the spirit*
	lifts, soaring / . . .

Italics, Bold and Underlining

As tools for separating, highlighting and clarifying printed matter, these devices are on the margins of punctuation. Although they can hardly apply to handwritten prose, in this word-processing age the *italic*, **bold** and underline keys make possible a range of typographic effects. Most have been used in this book:

FOR EMPHASIS	Do **not** use a capital letter after a colon.

TO DISTINGUISH A WORD OR WORD GROUP

Less than a century ago, <u>tomorrow</u> was hyphenated as <u>to-morrow</u>.

TO IDENTIFY AN EXTRACT OR QUOTATION

The Collins English Dictionary describes an adjective as **a word imputing a characteristic to a noun or pronoun**.

TO INDICATE TITLES

Several errors involving quotation marks will be found in Jane Austen's *Persuasion*.

TO INDICATE A FOREIGN WORD OR PHRASE

The movement's meetings were always heavy with *Sturm und Drang*, shouting and argument.

The building blocks of good writing: Grammar without grief

A preposition is not a good word to end a sentence with.
And remember to not ever split infinitives.

from *The Thirteen Gremlins of Grammar*

A language requires two keys to fulfil its role as a communication tool – a **vocabulary** and a **grammar**.

The vocabulary is a language's stock of words: combinations of symbols, signs and letters that have meanings that identify things and ideas. But words by themselves can never constitute a language, any more than a million loose tennis balls can form a vertical wall. What is needed is some glue or cement to stick them together. In the case of a language this glue is a mixture of rules called grammar.

To make sense of grammar it is difficult to avoid familiarity with at least a few basic terms. We will, however, keep these to a workable minimum.

The components that we use as building blocks for the way we speak and write are called the 'parts of speech', and we can identify most of them by analysing a sentence such as this one:

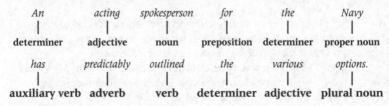

Now let's look a little closer at these grammatical building blocks.

Nouns are for naming things

Nouns make up by far the biggest family of words in the English language. This is because nouns name things; everything, everyone, almost every place in the universe has a name:

PLACES	*street, home, Germany, Paris, heaven*
OBJECTS	*plate, chair, tree, chamber pot, vapour*
PERSONS	*Einstein, Michael Jackson, Caroline*
ANIMALS	*pony, pig, chimp, whale, butterfly*
CONCEPTS	*option, bad temper, ability, direction*

We also recognise types of nouns. All names are nouns, but not all nouns are names. To make the distinction we use the terms **proper noun** for specific names, and **common noun** for nouns that are broadly descriptive:

PROPER NOUN	COMMON NOUN
Bentley	*car*
Boeing 747	*aircraft*
Hoover	*vacuum cleaner*
Britain	*country*
Agaricus campestris	*mushroom*
Madonna	*singer*
Easter	*holiday*

Nouns are always preceded by a **determiner**: an article such as *a, an* or *the*; pronouns such as *this, my, his*; or words which work as determiners such as *another, several, each, many, either, neither*, etc. This is a good way to find out if a word is a noun or not:

NOUN	NON-NOUN
a racehorse	*a racing*
the park	*the parked*
an assembly	*an assemble*
some cash	*some cashable*
her shampoo	*her shampooing*

Other tests include a noun's ability to take on singular and plural form (*book, books*); to be replaced by pronouns (*he, she, it*); and to accept add-ons to form new nouns (*book / a booking / booklet / bookman / bookmark*).

Nouns can be **concrete** nouns, entities we can detect with our senses (*earth, sky, girl, concrete*); and **abstract** nouns, which describe concepts, ideas and qualities (*team, instinct, strength, coincidence*).

Both common and proper nouns have gender, too:

	MASCULINE	**FEMININE**	**NEUTER**
Common nouns	*boy, bull, cock, man*	*woman, girl, hen*	*letter, box*
Proper nouns	*Frank Sinatra,*	*Joan of Arc,*	*Xerox, Rome*

Countable and Uncountable Nouns

Nouns can be further divided into **countable** and **uncountable** nouns. A countable noun is usually preceded by a determiner and can take either singular or plural form:

a hamburger	*five hamburgers*	*several hamburgers*
an egg	*a dozen eggs*	*a nest of eggs*
the mountain	*the two mountains*	*the range of mountains*

Uncountable nouns cannot be counted, nor do they have a plural form:

music, poetry, cement, light, luck, greed, clothing

Singular and Plural Nouns

A noun's capacity to exist in singular and plural forms causes problems for many writers not least because it is surrounded by inconsistencies. Some plural words have no singular: *scissors, knickers, marginalia*. Some words have singular and plural forms spelt the same: *shambles, congeries*. And here are a few more oddities:

mouse, mice	*loaf, loaves*	*tooth, teeth*	*foot, feet*
ox, oxen crisis, crises	*hoof, hooves*	*child, children*	*stimulus, stimuli*
medium, media	*larva, larvae*	*index, indices*	

But such inconsistencies aside, most nouns change from singular to plural by the simple addition of an *s* (*shop, shops*) or an *es* (*bush, bushes; circus, circuses*).

Collective Nouns

Collective nouns are very useful but can cause a lot of confusion. They unify things, ideas, animals or people into groups:

audience, the Government, council, team, jury, orchestra

The effect of a collective noun is to create a singular entity which, although many people (*sailors in a navy*), animals (*bees in a swarm*) or things (*plants in a crop*) are involved, should be treated as a singular noun:

The Army is outside the city gates.
Will this class please behave itself!
The committee is still deliberating.

Unfortunately we can't leave it there, because many collective nouns refuse to be straitjacketed. They can simply break the singular rule and demand to be treated as plurals! How? Look at this sentence in which *family* is the collective noun:

The family was given just a week to find a new home.

Here the family is treated as a single entity and is therefore followed by a singular verb – *was*. But there are times when a family can be seen more as a number of individual members:

The family were informed that if their anti-social behaviour continued, they would be evicted.

In this case the writer assumes that the members of the family were not necessarily consulted or warned as a single entity, but individually – not an unreasonable assumption. Accordingly, *family* requires a plural verb and pronouns. In most newspapers today you will find that, increasingly, collective nouns such as *committee, team, jury, government,* are invariably treated as plural, regardless of the sense and context. Good writers, however, should always apply the 'family test' as in the case above, before committing to one or the other. In many cases your 'ear' will tell you: *a lot of things is wrong with the world today* may be grammatically correct but it sounds odd and most writers would replace *is* with *are*.

You, I, me, them and other Pronouns

Pronouns are versatile substitutes for nouns and noun phrases. Although perhaps a bit academic, it's worth running through the various kinds of pronouns to see what they do:

● **Personal Pronouns** We use these constantly to identify ourselves and others, in three ways:

- In the first person, the most intimate, which includes the person or persons doing the speaking or writing: *I, me, we, us, myself, ourselves.*
- In the second person, which embraces those who are being addressed: *you, yourself, yourselves.*
- In the third person, those or the things being spoken or written about – 'all the others': *he, him, she, her, it, they, them, themselves, itself.*
- The indefinite pronoun *one* can act as a substitute for the personal pronoun *I* as in *One is always being invited to openings;* or the average or generic person, as in *One can be the victim of aggressive neighbours without any reason.* Most users of English tend to regard either use as affected, but it can sometimes lend a certain elegance to an expression.

With the exception of *it*, which refers to things (although sometimes babies and animals), all personal pronouns refer to people, while *them* can refer either to people or things. There are some odd exceptions such as a ship, which is traditionally regarded not as an *it* but as a *she* or a *her*.

● **Possessive Pronouns** These indicate possession or ownership and are sometimes called possessive adjectives. Some are used as determiners, and are dependent on nouns:

> *my* groceries, *her* hairdresser, *his* anger, *our* house, *your* face, *their* car

The other possessive pronouns are used on their own:

> it is *ours*, it is *mine*, *theirs* was stolen, *his* is that one, *hers* is green.

● **Reflexive Pronouns** This tribe insinuates its members into our lives in various ways: *look after* ***yourself****, they keep to* ***themselves***. Others are ***itself****,* ***herself****,* ***himself****,* ***yourselves****,* ***myself****,* ***ourselves***. You can see here that reflexive pronouns are entities in themselves.

● **Demonstrative Pronouns** These help us to demonstrate something or to point to things: *I'll take* ***this****. I'll have* ***that****.* ***These*** *will do.* ***Those*** *are too stale.*

● **Interrogative Pronouns** Not surprisingly, these are used to introduce questions: *who, what, which, whose, whom*. When you use them, make sure they're followed by a question mark: ***Who*** *is she?* ***Which*** *one?* ***Whose*** *are those?* ***Whom*** *am I speaking to?*

● **Relative Pronouns** These are *that, which, who, whom* and *whose* and they are used to introduce relative or subordinate clauses, as in *The suit that he was supposed to mend is ruined*, and *I'd like to buy the shoes which I saw in Marks yesterday*. The only trouble here is that we are increasingly dropping such pronouns and writing instead, *The suit he was supposed to mend* and *the shoes I saw in Marks yesterday*.

● **Indefinite Pronouns** These are aptly named because the nouns they are supposed to refer to are either vague or unknown. They are a mixed bunch, but you will quickly spot a common bond: *all, any, every, each, some, one, both, either, neither, few, little, less, least, many, everyone, someone, no one, something, anybody, more, most*. The common bond is that they all have to do with quantity: *nothing at all, a little, some, or a lot.*

When using indefinite pronouns you might wish to remember these points:

- ● Note that *no one* is the only two-word pronoun
- ● Note that *little, less* and *much* should refer to uncountable nouns (*less* fat, not *less* calories; *a little* sugar, not *a little* cakes). *Fewer* and *many* can be used instead (*fewer than five items, many trolleys*).

● Note that *each, one, either, neither, someone, no one, something* and *anybody* are all singular.

When using pronouns . . .

Try to avoid using a pronoun when it results in confusion and ambiguity, as in this old chestnut:

If your baby has trouble digesting cow's milk, boil it.

Here the pronoun 'it'could refer to either noun (*baby, milk*) so although few mothers would boil the baby, the ambiguity is disconcerting. A rewrite might be:

If your baby has trouble digesting cow's milk, the milk should be boiled.

While pronouns referring to people are of either gender (*he, she*) or unspecified (*I, me, they*) there is an historical propensity to use masculine pronouns to refer to both sexes:

Any runner who does not finish will have his application for next year's marathon reconsidered by the race committee.

What about all the female runners? What does a writer do in this age of gender equality? One solution is to use the *his/her* formula (*Any runner who does not finish will have his or her application . . .*) but this is widely rejected as clumsy and is intensely irritating when repeated through a text. A more acceptable way is to pluralise the sentence: *Runners who do not finish will have their applications . . .*

The Business of Verbs

The business of verbs is to express action or to indicate a condition or state:

ACTION   *He is running away. She is breaking the engagement.*
STATE   *She loathes country music. He feels quite ill.*

Verbs also help us express time:

PAST   *He's been sacked. The car tipped over.*
PRESENT   *He's listening to her. He falls on the floor.*
FUTURE   *I will come tomorrow. He'll do it.*

Verbs are among the most versatile of all our words. You can see how productively functional they are in these two paragraphs. The first is a fairly matter-of-fact description:

Then the helicopter banked and almost stalled. The engines roared and the craft tilted and a body fell out of the hatch. The machine rapidly lost height and the engines died. Now only the wind could be heard. Then it began to revolve, falling out of control, throwing the pilot out of the cabin and finally plunging into the sea.

That could have been a report by an enquiry committee of a helicopter accident at sea. Here, though, is essentially the same passage, but brought graphically to life by selective verbs:

Suddenly the helicopter banked, shuddered, and seemed to stall, its arms rotating wildly, scrabbling and clawing the black sky for something to grip. The engines whined and screamed, the craft lurched and a body shot out of the hatch and hurtled into the void below. The machine was now losing height, dropping at an increasing rate until the engines abruptly died, their howling replaced by the eerie whistling of the wind. Then, slowly at first, the fuselage itself began to spin around the stilled rotors, gyrating faster and faster, whirling and spinning out of control, spiralling down through the tunnel of rushing air until, a few seconds after the pilot was hurled out of the cabin, the rotors disintegrated and the grey coffin plummeted into the wild black water.

You can easily see how certain verbs – *shuddered, rotating, scrabbling, clawing, whined, screamed, shot, hurtled, dropping, spin, gyrating, spiralling, hurled, disintegrated, plummeted* – contribute to this vivid, action-packed word-picture. To heighten the effect even more, some writers might move the verbs to the present tense, to give the reader a 'you are there now' feeling:

. . . then, slowly at first, the fuselage itself begins to spin . . . the rotors disintegrate and the grey coffin plummets into the . . .

Because verbs are so useful and versatile, it's worth finding out what they can do for your writing, and how you can put them to work.

Regular and Irregular Verbs

Verbs are divided into two groups: **regular**, or weak verbs, of which there are thousands, and slightly fewer than 300 **irregular**, or strong verbs. Regular verbs stick to certain rules, while irregular verbs live up to their name and are real wild cards, as you will see.

REGULAR VERBS	*laugh, look, advises, play, loved*
IRREGULAR VERBS	*begin, chosen, speak, froze, shrink*

The difference between these two groups is in their behaviour when they change to express **tense** or **time**: present and past time. Regular verbs follow a pattern: the basic form of the verb simply adds an -s, -ing or -ed to indicate a different time or mood:

BASIC FORM	*laugh, look, play, advise, push*
PRESENT	*laughs, looks, plays, advises, pushes*
PRESENT PARTICIPLE	*laughing, looking, playing, advising, pushing*
PAST PAST PARTICIPLE	*laughed, looked, played, advised, pushed*

Irregular verbs, however, can behave quite erratically:

BASIC FORM	*begin, choose, speak, freeze, shrink*
PRESENT	*begins, chooses, speaks, freezes, shrinks*
PAST	*began, chose, spoke, froze, shrank*
PRESENT PARTICPLE	*beginning, choosing, speaking, freezing, shrinking*
PAST PARTICIPLE	*begun, chosen, spoken, frozen, shrunk*

Irregular verbs trouble writers because they can change in such unexpected ways:

> *If we speak, then we have spoken.*
> *But if we sneak, we have not snoken,*
> *And shoes that squeak have never squoken!*

Some verbs have three forms; *be* has ten! Here are some of the most lethal of these verbal tripwires:

Some Disorderly, Disobedient, Deviating Irregular Verbs!

BASIC	PRESENT	PAST	PRESENT PARTICPLE	PAST PARTICIPLE
arise	*arises*	*arose*	*arising*	*arisen*
awake	*awakes*	*awoke*	*awaking*	*awoken*
bear	*bears*	*bore*	*bearing*	*borne*
bid	*bids*	*bad(e)*	*bidding*	*bidden*
bite	*bites*	*bit*	*biting*	*bitten*
blow	*blows*	*blew*	*blowing*	*blown*
bring	*brings*	*brought*	*bringing*	*brought*
choose	*chooses*	*chose*	*choosing*	*chosen*
dive	*dives*	*dived*	*diving*	*dived*
do	*does*	*did*	*doing*	*done*
drive	*drives*	*drove*	*driving*	*driven*
fly	*flies*	*flew*	*flying*	*flown*
forgive	*forgives*	*forgave*	*forgiving*	*forgiven*
freeze	*freezes*	*froze*	*freezing*	*frozen*
go	*goes*	*went*	*going*	*gone*
hang	*hangs*	*hung/hanged*	*hanging*	*hung/hanged*
kneel	*kneels*	*kneeled/knelt*	*kneeling*	*knelt/kneeled*

BASIC	PRESENT	PAST	PRESENT PARTICPLE	PAST PARTICIPLE
lay	*lays*	*laid*	*laying*	*laid*
lie (recline)	*lies*	*lay*	*lying*	*lain*
lie (to tell a)	*lies*	*lied*	*lying*	*lied*
mistake	*mistakes*	*mistook*	*mistaking*	*mistaken*
quit	*quits*	*quit/quitted*	*quitting*	*quit/quitted*
sew	*sews*	*sewed*	*sewing*	*sewn*
shear	*shears*	*sheared*	*shearing*	*shorn/sheared*
shoe	*shoes*	*shoed/shod*	*shoeing*	*shod*
slay	*slays*	*slew*	*slaying*	*slain*
speed	*speeds*	*speeded/sped*	*speeding*	*sped/speeded*
spell	*spells*	*spelled/spelt*	*spelling*	*spelt/spelled*
steal	*steals*	*stole*	*stealing*	*stolen*
stink	*stinks*	*stank*	*stinking*	*stunk*
strew	*strews*	*strewed*	*strewing*	*strewn*
stride	*strides*	*strode*	*striding*	*stridden*
strike	*strikes*	*struck*	*striking*	*struck*
strive	*strives*	*strove*	*striving*	*striven*
tear	*tears*	*tore*	*tearing*	*torn*
thrive	*thrives*	*thrived*	*thriving*	*thrived*
tread	*treads*	*trod*	*treading*	*trodden/trod*
undergo	*undergoes*	*underwent*	*undergoing*	*undergone*
undo	*undoes*	*undid*	*undoing*	*undone*
wake	*wakes*	*waked/woke*	*waking*	*woken*
wet	*wets*	*wet/wetted*	*wetting*	*wet/wetted*
wring	*wrings*	*wrung*	*wringing*	*wrung*

Auxiliary Verbs

These are a group of words which, added to a main verb to form a verb phrase, enable us to express an amazing range of meanings. And by following an auxiliary with *not*, we can express a similar range of negatives. Let's track the main verb *speak* through a range of possibilities:

I speak	I **do not** speak
she **does** speak	she **does not** speak
she **is** speaking	she **is not** speaking
she **has** spoken	she **has not** spoken
she **has been** speaking	she **has not been** speaking
she **did** speak	she **did not** speak
she **had** spoken	he **had not** spoken
she **had been** speaking	she **had not been** speaking
she **will** speak	she **will not** speak
she **will be** speaking	she **will not be** speaking

. . . and so on. To these variations you can add a *must speak, may speak, might speak, shall speak, should speak,* etc series. Even these can be modified with *ought to speak, used to speak, had better speak, would rather speak* . . . the permutations are almost endless. It's astonishing, isn't it? And it certainly demonstrates how verbs, aided by their auxiliaries, can offer us so many shades of meaning with such economy.

Transitive and Intransitive Verbs

An **intransitive** verb can stand alone (*she speaks; he runs; I smile; the clock strikes*) while nearly all **transitive** verbs won't work unless they have some sort of relationship (*he raised his fist; she laid the book on the bed*). You can readily see that you can't just *raise* – you have to *raise something* – a glass, a shovel, an eyebrow, a laugh – something. Some verbs can be transitive and intransitive. A person can *breathe*, as in:

*That smoke was awful – at last I can **breathe**!*

In that sentence *breathe* is an intransitive verb. But here is the same word used as a dependent, transitive verb, which alters the meaning:

*I wish I could **breathe** some confidence into that pupil.*

Phrasal Verbs or Verb Phrases

We have seen how auxiliary verbs can form **verb phrases**. But verb phrases can also incorporate **prepositions** or **adverbs**: *look up, look out, look after, look for, give up, take off, look forward to, fall out, turn down.*

You'll probably note that all these examples have an idiomatic feel about them. If we hear someone say, 'She loves to run down her in-laws' we don't jump to the conclusion that she's trying to kill them with her car. The same applies to such expressions as 'Do you think Mary will run up a pair of curtains for me?'

Although many verb phrases acquire precise meanings (there's a big difference between *checking the speedometer* and *checking up on your husband*) many seem to add nothing except paradox to the original verb (*shout down, settle up, go back on, ring up*) but not even gelignite will stop us from using them.

Describing things: Adjectives and Adverbs

Adjectives define and modify nouns while **adverbs** do the same for nouns and verbs. They are close relations in a very big family of words and are often difficult to tell apart; so that when we use them we're inclined to abuse them. So it's a good idea to know something about adjectives and adverbs and how to use them to better effect.

Here's a sentence which depends almost entirely on adjectives and adverbs for its meaning:

*You're buying the **best**,*	**ADJECTIVE**
most	**ADVERB**
expensive,	**ADJECTIVE**
exciting	**PARTICIPLE**
and arguably	**ADVERB**
highest performance	**ADJECTIVE / NOUN**
saloon	**NOUN / ADJECTIVE**
car	**NOUN**

There are four kinds of modifier in that sentence: two adjectives, two adverbs, a **participle** (the verb *excite* used adjectivally by adding *-ing*), and two nouns (*performance, saloon*) also used in an adjectival way.

If both adjectives and adverbs are used to describe things and situations, how do you tell them apart? It's important to know this, as they are used quite differently and many writers fall down the gap in the middle.

Many adverbs can be identified by their *-ly* endings but there are also many without, and there are also some adjectives with *-ly* endings. Hence the confusion. But look at the different ways in which they are used:

ADJECTIVES	**ADVERBS**
He is a slow driver	*He drives slowly*
She is an early riser	*She rises early*
That's very loud music	*He's playing loudly*
He reads a daily newspaper	*He reads a newspaper daily*

When you see a road sign that commands you to *GO SLOW* and you sense that it should read *GO SLOWLY*; or hear someone say 'That feels real great!' and know that it should be not *real* (adjective) but *really* (adverb), then you've made good headway in your ability to use these grammatical tools correctly.

Adjectives

Here are some adjectives in use to show you how free-ranging they are:

DESCRIBING SIZE	*It was a **huge** marquee.*
DESCRIBING COLOUR	*The carpet was **red**.*
DESCRIBING A QUALITY	*I loved the **plush** armchairs.*
DEFINING QUANTITY	*There were **five** windows.*
DEFINING SPECIFICITY	*Did you see her **Persian** rug?*

. . . and so on.

Adjectives can be used liberally:

*What impressed Jeanne most of all were the **three big ancient green-tinged metallic Burmese religious** figures.*

119

Yes, it's a bit over the top, but here we have no fewer than seven adjectives, all adding something to the detailed description of the figures. With such an adjectival pile-up it helps to have your adjectives in some order. If we rewrite that sentence as:

What impressed Jeanne most of all were the **Burmese religious three big green-tinged ancient metallic** *figures.*

you should quickly discern that something's wrong. That's why we follow a generally accepted rule-of-thumb for arranging adjectives:

QUANTITY	*five, a hundred, a dozen*
EMOTIVE	*lovely, ugly, rare, repulsive*
SIZE	*large, tiny, six-foot*
AGE	*old, brand new, youngish*
COLOUR, TEXTURE	*blue, smooth, shiny, transparent*
SPECIFICITY	*Jewish, Japanese, photocopied*
PURPOSE	**wine** *glasss,* **dining** *table*

which, followed to the letter, might result in something like this:

The catalogue listed **two exquisite 23in 18th century silver Peruzzi candle** *holders.*

So, what makes an adjective? A lot of them are original descriptive words such as *good, dark* and *hot,* many of which have their opposites: *bad, fair* and *cold.*

But thousands more began life as nouns and verbs and were changed into adjectives by having endings tacked on to them. These are fairly easy to recognise as adjectives:

-able	*notable, fashionable, detestable, desirable*
-ible	*sensible, comprehensible, horrible, responsible*
-al	*natural, mortal, skeletal, oriental*
-ar	*jocular, circular, spectacular, singular*
-ed	*excited, crooked, married, cracked*
-ent	*excellent, indulgent, emergent, deficient*
-esque	*picturesque, Romanesque, statuesque*
-ful	*wonderful, hopeful, forgetful, thoughtful*
-ic	*heroic, psychic, angelic, romantic*
-ical	*periodical, magical, farcical, psychological*
-ish	*childish, liverish, quirkish, squeamish*
-ive	*reflective, massive, defensive, offensive*
-less	*endless, cloudless, hopeless, childless*
-like	*ladylike, lifelike, childlike*
-ous	*nervous, herbaceous, piteous, officious*

-some	*meddlesome, awesome, loathsome, fearsome*
-worthy	*newsworthy, praiseworthy, seaworthy*

but be on your guard with the two endings -ly and -y:

-ly	*lonely, crinkly, sickly, prickly*
-y	*earthy, shaky, funny, tacky, kinky*

. . . because these two endings share between them an obstacle course of pitfalls and booby traps. Try to separate the adjectives from the adverbs:

> *truly, idly, gravelly, loyally, woolly, yearly, holy, thankfully,*
> *gentlemanly, brazenly, properly*

If you try placing each of the words before a noun (*truly car, gravelly voice*) you should score an easy 100%. The adjectives are *gravelly, woolly, yearly, holy* and *gentlemanly*; the rest are adverbs (but did you remember that *yearly* can also double as an adverb?).

Kinds of Adjectives

Some adjectives can rove around a sentence with a certain amount of freedom while others are locked into fixed positions. The former are called **central adjectives** and the latter are **peripheral adjectives**. Here they are in use:

CENTRAL ADJECTIVE	*This is a new car.*
	This car is new.
	New the car may be, but I don't want it.
PERIPHERAL ADJECTIVE	*The man spoke utter nonsense.*

Here you see that the adjective *utter* can't be moved to any other position (*The man spoke nonsense that was utter?*); its function here as an adjective is specifically to qualify the noun *nonsense*. For different degrees of nonsense we could have used adjectives such as *absolute, puerile* or *childish*; instead we've settled for the old cliché which does the job well enough.

The Expanding Adjective

One of the most valuable services that adjectives provide is a range of comparisons. Imagine trying to describe the comparative size of objects – three mountains, saucepans, skyscrapers – without having recourse to the adjectives *small/smaller/smallest* or *large/larger/largest*. Most adjectives work like that: they can express several comparative degrees: the same, less, least, more, most. In some cases we add *-er* (*taller, weaker*) or *est* (*tallest, weakest*); while in others we qualify the adjective with *more* (*more entertaining*), *most* (*most endearing*), *less* (*less enthusiastic*) or *least* (*the least likely*). All these adjectival devices enable us to describe the size and scale of almost anything, any action, any feeling:

It was a big celebration. It was a very big celebration. It was the biggest celebration ever. It was bigger than any other celebration I've seen. It was a fairly big celebration. It was quite a big celebration. Well, it was a biggish celebration . . .

Adverbs

As with adjectives, we use **adverbs** to add information and extra layers of meaning to a statement. Adverbs, however, are even more versatile; while adjectives can dress up nouns and pronouns, adverbs can modify a verb here, boost an adjective there, appear in disguise to support another adverb – even boss whole phrases and sentences about!

First, let's take another look at adjectives and adverbs that can be mistaken for each other. Note again their placement and the way in which they work:

ADJECTIVES   *They caught the early train. He drew a long line.*
ADVERBS   *The train arrived early. She hadn't long left home.*

How Adverbs work

Here's a short catalogue of how we can use adverbs to add information and meaning:

DEFINING HOW   *The children played **happily** together.*
DENOTING PLACE   *They can play over **there**.*
FIXING TIME   *We can all go there **afterwards**.*
EXPRESSING GRADATION   *We never seem to see **enough**.*
EXPRESSING FREQUENCY   *We **never** go there.*
INDICATING VIEWPOINT   *I would never go there, **personally**.*
INDICATING ATTITUDE   ***Curiously**, she has never been there.*
LINKING A PREVIOUS   ***Nevertheless**, I feel we should go.*
THOUGHT

You'll note that some of the adverbs are stand-alone adverbs (*there, afterwards, enough,* etc), while others (*happily, personally* and *curiously*) have been created from existing words. The most common of these constructions is the *-ly* suffix (*historically, romantically*); other suffixes include *-wise* (*otherwise, clockwise*), *-wards* (*backwards, homewards*); and *-ways* (*endways, always*).

Positioning your Adverbs

In terms of using them in a sentence, adverbs offer a lot of options. The eminent linguist David Crystal has demonstrated the amazing all-purpose quality of many adverbs with devastating effect, using a seven-way sentence:

1. *Originally, the book must have been bought in the store.*
2. *The book originally must have been bought in the store.*
3. *The book must originally have been bought in the store.*
4. *The book must have originally been bought in the store.*
5. *The book must have been originally bought in the store.*
6. *The book must have been bought originally in the store.*
7. *The book must have been bought in the store originally.*

Not all adverbs are so flexible, however; many feel uncomfortable in certain positions while others, wrongly placed, can produce ambiguity and even hilarity. This rough guide should make you aware of such adverbial problems:

DEFINING MANNER (adverb usually at the end of sentence)
    NOT ADVISED   *He rather erratically walked.*
    MUCH BETTER   *He walked rather erratically.*

DENOTING PLACE (adverb typically at the end of sentence)
    NOT ADVISED   *Over there he threw the stone.*
    MUCH BETTER   *He threw the stone over there.*

FIXING TIME (adverb best towards the end of sentence)
    NOT ADVISED   *I recently saw that movie.*
    MUCH BETTER   *I saw that movie recently.*

EXPRESSING GRADATION (adverb works best in the middle)
    NOT ADVISED   *The jar is full, almost.*
    MUCH BETTER   *The jar is almost full.*

INDICATING FREQUENCY (adverb usually not at beginning)
    NOT ADVISED   *Always he is going to the pub.*
    MUCH BETTER   *He is always going to the pub.*

DENOTING ATTITUDE (adverb most effective at the beginning)
    NOT ADVISED   They both decided to wisely stay away.
    MUCH BETTER   Wisely, they both decided to stay away.

INDICATING VIEWPOINT (adverb best placed at front of sentence)
    NOT ADVISED   I shouldn't comment, strictly speaking.
    MUCH BETTER   Strictly speaking, I shouldn't comment.

A guide like this is not a rule book, for there are many exceptions. For example, *enough* is an adverb of gradation or degree and it is commonly placed in the middle of a sentence: *I've done enough work for the day*. But see what happens when *enough* is placed at the beginning and end of sentences: *Do you think they've had enough? Enough has been said on the subject already*. What has happened is that in both these examples *enough* had turned into a noun! Look at the sentences again and you will see that this is so.

Tips on using Adverbs

Carelessly shifting the position of adverbs can lead to ambiguity by altering the sense of the sentence:

James almost passed all his exam papers.
James passed almost all his exam papers.

We have to wonder, did James *almost pass all his exam papers* (i.e. he passed none of them) or *almost all of his exam papers* (i.e. not all, but most of them)?

One of the most contentious of such adverbial misplacements is the so-called **split infinitive** in which, typically, an adverb or adverbial phrase finds its way between the preposition *to* and a basic verb form:

to dearly love   *to properly understand*   *to boldly go*

Although still frowned upon by many grammarians and conscientious writers the split infinitive is considered allowable when clumsiness or ambiguity is caused by sticking to the rules. Two well-known examples are *failing completely to recognise* and *failing to completely recognise*, which have two completely different meanings.

Can you begin a sentence with an adverb? *Interestingly*, you can, but *The Times* cautions its journalists against it; this sentence is an example. 'Such constructions,' advises The Times, 'are not forbidden, but sentences starting with adverbs are normally built on sand.'

And a final tip: avoid 'neutralising adverbs'. Such phrases as *faintly repulsive*, **rather** *appalling*, *pretty ugly*, **somewhat** *threatening* and **slightly** *lethal* cancel out the intended effect. Such an oxymoronic habit should be *gently stamped out.*

Grammatical Glue

We come now to the group of words with which we construct all our writing and speech. Without them, and using only nouns, verbs, adjectives and adverbs, our sentences would look very strange and probably indecipherable. These grammatical elements, which you probably remember vaguely but can't quite recall, are **determiners**, **conjunctions** and **prepositions**. They all play important roles in communicating, acting as a kind of grammatical glue.

Determiners

Determiners precede and determine certain qualities of nouns and noun phrases. In the attributive sense, they act as adjectives. Here's a list of the kind of determiners we use most frequently. The first five kinds, known as **definites,** are used to indicate that the noun is personal or specific:

DEFINITE ARTICLE	*I will buy **the** car. He will see **the** car.*
POSSESSIVE	*It is **my** car. It is **his** car.*
POSSESSIVE PROPER	*It is **Jenny's** car. It is **Lyn's** car.*
DEMONSTRATIVE	*I want **that** car. She bought **this** car.*
NUMBER	*You have **two** cars? No, just **one** car.*

The next group of determiners are called indefinites because they generalise or merely broadly qualify nouns:

INDEFINITE ARTICLE	*I saw **a** great movie. She ate **an** apple.*
QUANTIFIER	*She saw **every** movie. I saw **most** movies.*
EXCLAMATORY	***What** a movie! It was **such** a great movie!*
INTERROGATIVE	***Which** movie? **Whose** ticket did you use?*

Most of us possess an easy familiarity with such words. We know not to use two determiners together: *I will buy **the a** car. Did you see **some several** movies?* We also soon learn to drop following nouns: *I saw **them all** (movies). Lyn bought **both** (cars).* With our ears and instinct most of us experience very few problems with determiners.

Conjunctions

Conjunctions are very strong glue because they're used to link parts of a sentence together:

She plays the violin and also the piano.

In this example, *and* is the conjunction that coordinates both parts of the sentence. It is the simplest kind of conjunction in that it is a link and nothing more; it adds no new information to the sentence. In fact, you could turn it right round without altering the meaning:

She plays the piano and also the violin.

But there are other conjunctions that, while gluing the sentence together, can also impart extra meaning:

She likes the piano, but the violin is her favourite.

Conjunctions are usually grouped according to the meaning they add:

EXPRESSING	SOME EXAMPLES	TYPICAL USAGE
TIME	***before, after, until, since,***	*She'll come home **after** lunch.*
PLACE	***where, wherever***	*I'll find out **where** it is.*
CAUSE	***since, because, as, for***	*I feel ill **because** I ate too much*

CONDITION	*if, although, unless, or*	*I'll feel better **if** I lie down.*
COMPARISON	*as, than, like, as, if,* *as though*	*It looks **as though** it will rain.*
CONTRAST	*although, while,* *whereas*	*I'm good at English **while*** *Emily is best at maths.*
PURPOSE	*so that, so as to, in* *order that*	*I must stop **so as to** let some of* *the others speak.*
RESULT	*so, so that, such that*	*He shouted **so that** they could* *hear*
PREFERENCE	*sooner than, rather* *than*	*I'd eat worms **rather than** go* *hungry.*
EXCEPTION	*except, except that,* *excepting that*	*He'd play, **except that** he's just* *just torn a muscle.*

Prepositions, and where to put them

About the only thing most people know about **prepositions** is that you shouldn't end a sentence with one. But of greater importance is mastering the subtelties of this irksome but indispensable group of words.

A preposition usually acts as a linking word, like a conjunction, but it also relates one part of a sentence to the other:

We went	*to*	*the beach.*
June rose	*at*	*the unusual hour of 5 am.*

From these two examples you will have noticed the preposition's particular ability to unite separate statements in terms of space (*to*) and time (*at*). We could also go *near the beach, on the beach,* or *beside,* or *along the beach.* In each case a preposition is giving us an important spatial clue. To clarify the point, here are some common prepositions:

SPACE	*between, above, over, into, near, beside, along, on*
TIME	*until, since, past, before, after, at, during*
OTHERS	*as, for, in, to, by, with, without*
MULTI-WORD	*instead of, other than, in front of, up to*

An interesting thing about prepositions is that when you use one in a sentence, it can only be replaced by another preposition. Try it:

> *She found a mouse in the house.*
> *She found a mouse near the house.*
> *She found a mouse under the house . . .* and so on.

Only with great difficulty could you substitute any other class of words – say, adjectives, adverbs, determiners, nouns or verbs. You might say that a preposition is like the keystone of an arch: take it away, and . . .

Problems with Prepositions

There are three problems with prepositions. The first is that we tend to create long-winded ones when short ones are freely available. Here are some of the former, with suggested replacements:

as a consequence of (because of)	*in addition to (besides)*
in the course of (during)	*with a view to (to)*
in excess of (more than)	*in case of (if)*
for the purpose of (to)	*prior to (before)*
for the reason that (because)	*subsequent to (after)*
in the neighbourhood of (about)	*in order to (to)*
in the nature of (like)	*in the event of (if)*

The second problem with prepositions is the ancient one already referred *to*. That is, as in the previous sentence, allowing a sentence to end with a preposition. The modern view is that if such a sentence looks and sounds comfortable the offending preposition should stay. If it jars, rewrite it. The sentence above doesn't jar but if you are determined not to be a 'preposition ender' you might write, *The second problem with prepositions is the ancient one to which we've already referred*. If the sentence resembles in any way Churchill's famous jibe at some civil servant's memo – 'This is the sort of English up with which I will not put' – then you'd certainly rewrite it.

The third problem with prepositions is that the lazier among us are tending to drop them altogether: *Defenestration means throwing someone out the window* should read, *out of the window*. Dropping prepositions is, needless to say, a habit that should be discouraged and offenders should be *defenestrated*.

Writing elegant, expressive English: The elements of style

The apples on the tree are full of wasps;
Red apples, racing like hearts. The summer pushes
Her tongue into the winter's throat.

from *The Pelt of Wasps* by David Constantine

We've been lectured on shoddy workmanship. We've been hammered on grammar and punctuation. We've worked like navvies with the nuts and bolts and girders of the language. We've done the hard labour.

Now the paint job, to cover all the construction. The magic bit, when at last you're allowed to throw the verbs and nouns in the air and juggle the adverbs and adjectives to produce some inspirational prose, and – *Pouf!* Well, perhaps we're not quite there yet.

So far we've concerned ourselves with what is correct and acceptable and advised and what is not. All that information will, in various ways, contribute something towards your writing style. But now we're going to look at style in its broadest sense, examining the elements that help to hide the hard labour. One of the greatest stylists in English, Somerset Maugham, put it this way: 'A good style should show no sign of effort. What is written should seem a happy accident'.

Another eminent stylist, the novelist and playwright Keith Waterhouse, noted that although there have been great blind writers, from Homer to Milton and beyond, there have been no great deaf ones in the sense of 'being unable to hear one's composition in one's head, as Beethoven heard his music'. Waterhouse insisted that while the mind dictates what is to be written, the ear monitors what is going down on paper – or at least it should. Writers with a tin ear are never likely to write with precision, brevity and elegance – or with style.

Just as certain blends of musical notes stir us deeply in some mysterious way, so certain combinations of words possess the strange power to freeze us in our tracks, to inspire us, to echo in our minds for a lifetime. How is it done? Of course, everbody would like to know. But for the present we are earthbound, dependent still on our box of grammatical tricks for the magic. Some writers – perhaps you – will transcend the box of tricks and create real magical prose, but at least the rest of us have the opportunity to learn to write good, crisp, clear English, which is no mean accomplishment.

Style is the way in which writers use the language to express themselves. The three-line excerpt from a poem at the beginning of this chapter evokes an autumnal mood with a combination of words that is unique to that writer. Unless we allow the most bizarre coincidence, no other writer on earth, no matter how much he or she learns about grammar and style, will at any time now or in the future throw those words together in that particular way.

Meanwhile, though, we should be getting on with the job – polishing, burnishing, simplifying, colouring our writing, developing a critical ear and learning from writers who please and thrill us, practising our box of tricks.

Remember the Basics

Achieving good writing is a learning process. And like all learning, start with the simple. In our case, start with simple, clear prose – no pyrotechnics, no words or expressions you don't quite understand – just tell it like it is. Take Dr Samuel Johnson's advice, quoting what an old college tutor said to a pupil: 'Read over your compositions, and wherever you meet with a passage which you think is particularly fine, strike it out'.

Plain writing need not be dull writing. On the contrary, a good writer always keeps the reader foremost in mind, thinking constantly, 'Will the reader grasp what I'm writing . . . enjoy reading it . . . laugh at this joke . . . learn something? If the warning bell rings a good writer unhesitatingly changes a word, switches a phrase around, rewrites and reviews again . . . and again. Sounds like hard work. But the end product is worth it and can be very satisfying.

Go down to the 'word gym' and practise some exercises. Writing directions will get rid of the flab. Try writing directions for tying a granny knot. Or how to drive a car, or make a cheese omelette. Every good writer needs some humility!

Build on Brevity

The Americans Strunk and White, in their 20 million copy best-seller *The Elements of Style*, distilled an essay on the beauty of brevity into one paragraph:

> *Vigorous writing is concise. A sentence should contain no unnecessary words, a paragraph no unnecessary sentences, for the same reason that a drawing should have no unnecessary lines and a machine no unnecessary parts. This requires not that the writer make all his sentences short, or that he avoid all detail and treat his subjects only in outline, but that every word tell.*

By brevity we do not mean the extreme terseness of telegram-speak. That can rebound, as a showbiz reporter once discovered when he wired the actor Cary Grant, then in his sixties: 'How old Cary Grant?' The actor replied, 'Old Cary Grant fine'.

Few people these days want to write more words than necessary, or to be forced to read two hundred words when the information could have been conveyed in a hundred.

Earlier we saw how, by combining simple sentences into compound sentences, we can economise on words and even enhance clarity; but there is another grammatical convention that allows us to trim away words we don't need, or 'sentence fat'. It's called **ellipsis**, and it works like this:

WITHOUT ELLIPSIS
When the children were called to the dinner table they came to the dinner table immediately.

WITH ELLIPSIS
When the children were called to the dinner table they came immediately.

The reason we get away with this trimming is that, if the reader is paying attention (or you, the writer, have won his or her attention!) he or she will automatically supply the missing words from the context of what is written.

Alexander Pope's advice on brevity is as sound today as it was nearly three centuries ago:

Words are like leaves; and where they most abound,
Much fruit of sense beneath is very rarely found.
Or, to further encapsulate the thought: lean is keen.

Change up a gear: Active and Passive

Would you rather do something, or have something done to you? With the first choice, you are in control; in the second you are the subject of somebody's whim. That's about the difference between what is known grammatically as the **active voice** and the **passive voice**. Being aware of the difference between active and passive expressions will make an enormous impact on your writing. Look at these sentences:

ACTIVE
*The favourite **won** the 3.30 hurdle event.*
*Her boyfriend **bought** the ring.*

PASSIVE
*The 3.30 hurdle event **was won** by the favourite.*
*The ring **was bought** by her boyfriend.*

It's easy to see why one kind of sentence is called active and the other passive; active sentences are direct and personal and seem more interesting, while passive sentences tend to be detached and impersonal by comparison.

If you are writing a scientific or academic article, then passive would be appropriate; otherwise use the active voice. And when you do, be careful not to slip into the passive mode, which will only result in discord:

> *My father painted those pictures which were left to me.*

That sentence begins with the active voice (*My father painted those pictures*) but then switches to the passive (*which were left to me*). What the sentence should have said is, *My father painted those pictures and left them to me.* Follow the logic: my father did both things – painted the pictures and (presumably) left them to me.

. . . and up a gear again

Mixing active and passive expressions isn't the only source of discord in a sentence. Perhaps the most prevalent form of discord is the sentence which fails to recognise that a singular noun takes a singular verb and a plural noun takes a plural verb:

WRONG   *We **was** furious with the umpire's decision.*
         *The four houses **isn't** for sale.*
CORRECT *We **were** furious with the umpire's decision.*
         *The four houses **aren't** for sale.*

These are glaringly apparent examples but less obvious traps lie in wait in longer sentences:

> *The Harris Committee has just a week (to January 17) to announce their initial findings.*

Clearly either *has/its* or *have/their* are required.

Shifting from personal to impersonal pronouns in the same sentence (and vice versa) is another common mistake:

> *If one is to keep out of trouble, you should mind your own business.*

Either stay with *one* or the personal (preferred) *you*.

Accentuating the positive (as they say) will vastly improve your writing style:

> *That dog is not unlike the one I saw in town yesterday.*
> *That dog is similar to the one I saw in town yesterday.*

Using the *not un-* construction is very fashionable today but if you heed George Orwell's advice (from his *Politics and the English Language* of 1946) you'll desist:

> *A not unblack dog was chasing a not unsmall rabbit across a not ungreen field.*

In fact it pays to have a 'not unuseful warning device' attached to your writing; too much negativism can have a depressing effect on the reader. Sometimes it is more tactful to express a negative thought in a positive way. *She is not beautiful* is negative and also vague: she could be *statuesque* or *handsome, obese* or *pimply*.

Add colour to your Word Palette

Are you conscious that you may be writing in monochrome? Without the vibrancy, the variety, the sensuality and fun of colour? Then what you need is a paintbox of verbal effects, a word palette of literary devices called figures of speech: **metaphor, simile, hyperbole, alliteration** and **wordplay**.

Metaphor

We're surrounded by everyday **metaphors**: *raining cats and dogs, mouth of the river, stony silence, he sailed into him, over the moon* . . . thousands of them are irrevocably part of the language. The difficulty is in inventing new ones, and writers who can, and can inject them at appropriate places in their texts, are a step ahead of the rest of us.

The beauty of metaphor is that it has the ability to bring a dull expression vividly to life, and explain a difficult concept with startling clarity. We still use Dickens's 'The law is an ass' probably because nobody else has come up with a better pithy description for the odd and illogical decisions that can issue from our courts.

As you can see, metaphor is describing something by using an analogy with something quite different. If we hear that a person 'has egg on his face' we are expected to know that he wasn't the victim of a phantom egg-thrower, but has been left in a very embarrassing situation. *Egg* and *embarrassment* are connected only by *a wild flight of imagination* (metaphor and cliché!).

By all means invent new metaphors but try to avoid creaky old ones. And in particular, watch out for mixed metaphors such as *They were treading in uncharted waters* and *I smell a rat but I'll nip him in the bud.*

Simile

A **simile** makes a direct comparison between two dissimilar things: *as fit as a fiddle, as good as gold, as sick as a parrot, he's crazy like a fox, ears like jug handles.* You'll note that invariably similes are introduced by the conjunction *as* or the preposition *like*.

A simile can enliven a piece of writing, but it should preferably be original; as with metaphors, creating apt similes is a special art. If your skill is on a par with that of Robert Burns (*My love is like a red, red rose*), Wordsworth (*I wandered lonely as a cloud*) or Cecil Day Lewis (*a girl who stands like a questioning iris by the waterside*), or an anonymous Aussie (*she was all over me like a rash*) then have fun with similes. But most of us need to employ tired simile-avoidance techniques to prevent our writing being clogged by such hoary chestnuts as *sharp as a razor, dull as ditchwater, pleased as Punch, plain as a pikestaff* and *mad as a March hare.*

Hyperbole

Hyperbole is deliberate overstatement: wild exaggeration used to make an emphatic point. Someone who complains that *I'm dying of hunger* or *I could eat a horse* would probably be perfectly satisfied with a hamburger. A person who offers you *a thousand apologies* would be somewhat taken aback if you insisted on having them.

As with other figures of speech, hyperbole has to be witty or outrageous to succeed. It's a stylistic area that leaves us envious of the writers who first coined such hyperbolic classics as *I got legless last night; couldn't fight his way out of a paper bag; couldn't organise a piss-up in a brewery* and *a diamond that would choke a horse.*

If you think you can beat 'em, then join 'em.

Alliteration and Wordplay

Making mischief with words is a way of having fun with the language and it's something every writer feels the urge to do at some point. However, intruding drollery into prose can fall *as flat as a pancake* (**simile, cliché**) if it isn't up to scratch, and even when it is, it should be used sparingly.

Here are some more pastel shades you can squeeze on to your word palette.

● **Alliteration** *Sing a song of Sixpence* and *Peter Piper picked a peck of pickled peppers* are examples of alliteration from the nursery – the repetition of stressed sounds in words adjacent or near one another. Here's another example, in verse form, from the Gilbert and Sullivan opera, *The Mikado: To sit in solemn silence in a dull, dark dock / In a pestilential prison, with a life-long lock / Awaiting the sensation of a short, sharp shock / From a cheap and chippy chopper on a big, black block!*

Alliteration that's been clumsily shoe-horned into your writing will *stick out like a sore thumb* (simile, cliché) so don't strive for alliterative effect. Mellifluous alliteration involving at most two or three words in a sentence will, with the least assistance from you, often occur naturally if your writing is flowing well.

● **Colloquialism and Idiom** Knowing when and where to use colloquial, idiomatic and slang expressions is a matter of style and experience. Their occasional use can certainly take the stuffiness out of some writing. They include such expressions as *get cracking, don't drop your bundle, go for it, give us a break, it'll be all right on the night, d.i.y* (colloquialisms); *part and parcel, keep a straight face, pass the buck, how's tricks?, odds and ends* (idioms); *bimbo, ankle biter, sprog, muttonhead, ballbreaker, jollies, tosser* (slang).

● **Litotes** (pron. *ly*-toe-tees) Litotes is understatement, the opposite of hyperbole . . . so what's the point? Some examples may help: *this is no easy task, he was not a little upset, not uncommon, not a bad writer.* In other words litotes is a way of asserting a statement by denying its opposite: *not bad* means *good, fine, okay.* Litotes can convey fine shades of meaning, so use this device carefully; it can go off in your hand.

● **Synecdoche** This is a figurative device in which a part is substituted for the whole, or the whole for a part. Follow? Some examples: *We sent twenty head to France today.* (i.e. *We sent twenty cattle.* The expression uses part of the cow to indicate the whole). *England beat Australia by three wickets.* (Here the whole – *England and Australia* – is used to indicate a part – the English and Australian cricket teams). The device is useful in achieving brevity and avoiding repetition. One of the most common – and contentious – synecdochic expressions is *man*, which, in the sense of *mankind*, is only part of a whole, *man and woman.*

Don't come down with a crash!

Perhaps learning to write fluently is a bit like learning to fly. Once you experience the heady feeling of being airborne and solo, the sky's the limit. Barrel rolls, loops, dives, Immelmann turns, you can do it all. And maybe you can. But you can also stall, lose direction, run out of gas . . . even the most thoroughly trained flyer can have *a bad air day.* So learn to temper your new-found skills with caution.

Enough has been said about longwindedness, clichés, tautology, gobbledegook, jargon and euphemism for an amber light to flash every time you stray in their direction. But there are still a few more amber, if not red, light districts awaiting the adventurous but unwary writer.

● **Elegant Variation** In a review of a biography of Abraham Lincoln by David Donald, the novelist Martin Amis wrote: 'Although Donald may be as methodical as Lincoln, he is his junior not least in literary talent. The prose is continually defaced by that scurviest of all graces, Elegant Variation. Here is but one example of Donald's futile ingenuity: 'If the president seemed to support the Radicals in New York, in Washington he appeared to back the Conservatives.' Although many might think that Amis was being a bit picky, he was surely justified, in defending the principles of style, in criticising the author's obvious recourse to a 'strained synonym'; rather than repeat *seemed to support,* the author substituted *appeared to back.* This practice, abhorred by stylists, was first identified by the grammarian H W Fowler, who scornfully called it 'Elegant Variation'.

Every writer can face the problem of dealing with identical words appearing in the same sentence or an adjoining one. In writing dialogue, for example, the word *said* is likely to be endlessly repeated at the risk of annoying the reader. The quick solution is to substitute near-synonyms: *uttered, replied, responded, answered, retorted, remarked, announced, added,* etc. If such substitutions are used judiciously and with restraint, the reader will probably not realise what is going on; fluency and readability will not be impaired.

Running to the thesaurus or synonymn dictionary for a replacement word can trap the rookie writer who will proceed merrily, unaware of the smell left behind to be picked up by the fastidious reader. Rewriting the sentence might be a better solution, or even, if allowing the repeated word if doesn't jar, leaving it in.

● **Puns and Humour** Attempts at humour can be the downfall of the adventurous but incautious writer. Perhaps that's why there are very few writers able to make their readers laugh. Although newspapers will pay the earth for them, they still remain only a handful internationally. Are you likely to be one of them?

This is not to say that your writing should be uniformly po-faced. A light touch is appreciated by more readers and it is no bad thing to aim at being amusing from time to time. A well-placed witty turn of phrase, a funny but apt quotation, a waggish allusion or mischievous irony – all these are within reach of writers who may have to be hypercritical of their work.

Except for national tabloid headlines, puns are regarded with deep suspicion by many writers. They can be verbal banana skins. The pun towards the end of the opening paragraph of this section (*a bad air day* for *a bad hair day*, itself a metaphor) is a calculated risk, as all such puns must be.

● **Adjectival economy** In discussing adjectives, we demonstrated how they can be accumulated to form an accurate description of an object, person or idea. One example showed a pile-up of seven consecutive adjectives, which is rather too many.

Such overloading can cause confusion; by the time the reader has reached the last one the first may have been forgotten.

But, more importantly, make sure that every adjective you use adds something essential to the description: *Her skis sliced through the powdery white snow on her downward trajectory*. Most of us know that snow is white, and believe it is very difficult to ski uphill, so the adjectives *white* and *downward* could well be returned to the dictionary.

● **Plagiarism.** In their pursuit of rapid progress, some ambitious writers are led up the dodgy path of plagiarism – words, ideas, stories or texts copied from the work of other writers. Very few writers have the gall to copy a work in its entirety and claim it as their own, but it has been done. More common is the practice of 'borrowing' someone else's work without indicating this by the use of quotation marks, or crediting its source. This can lead to complaint and legal action: every year in Britain there is at least one serious – and sometimes costly – accusation of plagiarism.

As a cautionary tale, here is the case of two books, one a biography of the Empress Eugenie published in 1964 by Harold Kurtz, and the other about royal brides by the Princess Michael of Kent, published in 1986:

The Empress Eugenie Harold Kurtz	*Crowned in a Far Country* Princess Michael of Kent
All her life Eugenie placed very little importance on sex, not as something wicked, just unimportant and cheap. 'You mean,' she would say in tones of incredulity, 'that men are interested in nothing but that?' when her ladies were chatting about the infidelities of men.	*All her life Eugenie placed very little importance on sex; not as something wicked, just unimportant and cheap. 'You mean,' she would say in disbelief, 'that men are interested in nothing but that?' when her ladies were chatting about infidelities.*

On the face of it, this looks pretty incriminating. But do bear in mind that finding the same thought expressed by a later writer does not *necessarily* mean that the later writer has plagiarised the original. Coincidences do happen; and never forget that lawyers are always vigilant for rash accusations. All one can say is that there comes a point in the course of a book when it becomes obvious to all (even lawyers) that a later writer is simply copying what an earlier writer has written, so be warned about purloining prose! And if you have heard that there is no copyright in literary ideas, concepts, structure and titles, take care also, because if it can be proved that you are 'passing off' another's original work you could find yourself at the wrong end of a lawsuit.

To sum up . . .

- Brevity is beautiful. So is simplicity. Short words too. And short sentences.
- Prefer concrete to abstract words
- Prefer the active voice to the passive
- Prefer positive expressions to negative
- Keep sentences harmonious – in voice, tense and number
- Listen to your sentences
- Remember that it is your job to attract and keep the reader's attention
- Think precision
- Think poetry

Finding out : a word about dictionaries

Lexicographer, **n.** *[Lexicographe, French] A writer of dictionaries; a harmless drudge, who busies himself in tracing the original, and detailing the signification of words.*

Dr Johnson's *Dictionary of the English Language,* 1755

Although it is generally agreed that the first English dictionary was Robert Cawdrey's *A Table Alphabetical* of 1604, it was Dr Johnson's monumental *A Dictionary of the English Language* of 1755 that made the huge leap to establish English as the brilliant tool of communication that it is today. It was the most influential dictionary in the English-speaking world until the appearance of the *New English Dictionary* – later called the *Oxford* – between 1884 and 1928.

Nine years in the making, with the combined labours of Johnson and six helpers, the massive dictionary defined 43,000 words and became the ultimate reference book on English for a century and a half. Far from being a dry academic tome, Johnson's dictionary bristles with the author's personality, errors and inconsistencies, wonderfully concise definitions and – Johnson being Johnson – a few jokes. One of these was his definition of a dictionary maker (above); another was his definition of oats: A grain which in England is generally given to horses, but which in Scotland support the people. The Scots got their own back with the riposte: 'Johnson has explained why Scotland has the most beautiful women, and England the most beautiful horses'.

Dictionaries have, of course, come a long way since Dr Johnson's 6-kilo, leather bound compilation of 43,000 words.

A favourite among writers is the Collins family, the workhorse being the Concise of 1764 pages at around £17. The authority behind the Collins dictionaries is the unique COBUILD project which began with the creation of a completely new database of millions of words of modern English which is used to monitor daily usage of the language. With this backing, Collins claims to be the most up-to-date reference. Collins dictionaries also typically include encyclopaedic and proper noun entries which busy writers find extremely useful.

Another dictionary that claims to be bang up to date is Chambers 21st Century Dictionary (1,664 pages, about £18.90) and it has many supporters, especially 'Scrabble' addicts (it is the final authority for the acceptability of words for the game).

Other dictionaries which should be inspected before settling on this essential reference tool are the Oxford English Dictionary (1,696 pages, £16.99 hardback), and the Longman Dictionary of Contemporary English (1,668 pages, £13.50 softbound), among others.

Persisting with a battered old pocket dictionary is a waste of time. At the very least you should have a comprehensive, up-to-date middle-of-the-range dictionary (120,000+ definitions). You'll find it indispensable and at only around £15–20 there is absolutely no excuse for not having one.

A dictionary defines words; it does not usually explain how to use them although today many entries will give examples of usage. It **describes**, does not **prescribe**. For guidance on how to use words there are books on English usage; for helping you find the exact word you want there are synonym dictionaries and the thesaurus, both described later.

Searching for Synonyms: the Thesaurus

Back in 1852 an Anglo-Swiss doctor in Edinburgh, taking pity on 'those who are painfully groping their way and struggling with the difficulties of composition' published his now world-famous *Roget's Thesaurus of English Words and Phrases*. Since then, despite many influential detractors, it has sold some 35 million copies worldwide.

The contents of a thesaurus are arranged, not in alphabetical order, but according to the ideas they express. In Roget's book, words were divided into six classes: **abstract**, **space**, **matter**, **intellect**, **volition** and **affections**. These were further subdivided; **affections** was split up into **general**, **personal**, **sympathetic**, **moral** and **religious**. These headings were then reduced to a third division; for example under **moral** were listed **obligations**, **sentiments**, **conditions**, **practice** and **institutions**; and, finally, to a fourth layer.

Writers patient enough to familiarise themselves with *Roget* and similar thesauruses swear by this system of finding synonyms, but there are plenty of critics who regard this type of reference book (or CD) as nothing more than a bluffer's guide.

Because other more modern thesauruses have appeared, *Roget's* attempts to update itself every ten years or so. The result is a curious mix of archaic and often ephemeral contemporary slang words, giving rise to its reputation as a browsing book rather than a serious work of reference.

If you are not familiar with a thesaurus then by all means inspect one at a library or bookstore to see if you think one might be useful to you. But a quicker and more straightforward way into alternative words is a plain synonym dictionary. To use one of these effectively you must either know the word you wish to find a substitute for, or a word approximating its meaning. The words following the main entries of most synonym dictionaries overlap in shades of meaning, so with a little work you can usually find the word you want.

If the elusive word is missing from such an entry, the reader can select the one nearest to the meaning required and look that up; this cross-referencing process, the desired word can usually be found.

Most writers are inclined to defy the purists and have a good synonym dictionary on their desk. But use it with care and discretion and guard against that most despised of literary vices, **elegant variation**!

By constantly using dictionaries, you're bound to increase your vocabulary or word power, and the more words you know, and the better you know how and where to use them, the more effectively you'll be able to communicate.

HOW TO WRITE A BETTER LETTER

Say what you mean, get what you want

Communicate better with a well-written letter

In a man's letter his soul lies naked.

Dr Samuel Johnson

The Post Office in Britain handles over two billion items of personal correspondence a year; in the same period *The Times* receives just under an astonishing 100,000 letters from readers.

Telecommunications and electronic transmissions have risen exponentially, of course, but it would be a brave pundit who predicted the demise of letter writing. After all, faxes and e-mails still have to be written.

There may be a sound reason for the letter's lusty survival in the face of progress. A telephone call has the advantage of immediacy, with a minimum of preparation, but that is also its weakness. A letter allows the writer to weigh thoughts, plan strategies of approach and persuasion, withdraw cruel and rash statements, refine and sharpen arguments, and, having done all that, decide after a period of rumination not to send it at all. A well-written letter also allows the shy and retiring writer to stand tall alongside the silver-tongued telephone speaker. And there are other advantages. A letter is tangible; it carries weight, it is a record you can keep and it makes a pleasant change.

But a problem remains: the scourge of postman's block. What does one say? How does one say it? How does one coordinate paper, pen, envelope, stamp and address?

Let's face it: most of us are a bit rusty when it comes to writing letters. Some of us never really learnt. Once, it was normal for children who had received a gift to write a short, neat and closely supervised thank you letter to the benefactor; sadly, this is not so common nowadays. And even though we may rattle off chirpy letters to friends or relatives with ease, how do we suddenly change gear to plead for more time to pay an overdue account, or complain to neighbours about their barking dog, without causing World War Three; or write to an ombudsman seeking redress over bad pension advice?

The essence of an effective letter is its individuality; every letter, in wording and tone, must be unique to the circumstances and its recipient. So it can't be stressed enough that the sample letters that follow are simply guides to how various letter-writing problems might be tackled. Many have been adapted from real letters that achieved results, gleaned from colleagues, correspondents, companies and public institutions, but it would be a mistake to regard them as models to copy.

Preparation and Planning

Always have writing materials around the house; a pack of good-quality A4 lightly-lined bond paper if you write by hand, or standard bank, copier or computer paper if you use a word processor or typewriter; a supply of POP (Post Office Preferred) envelopes in a couple of sizes, 1st and 2nd class stamps. You will never carry through your self-improvement letter-writing plan if you have to concern yourself about materials every time.

Next, familiarise yourself with one of the accepted layouts for most letters:

The essentials are (**1**) your address (**2**) the date (**3**) the recipient's name and address.

The following can be dispensed with in personal letters to those you know well. (**4**) the introduction (**5**) the contents (**6**) the sign-off, your signature, and, in non-personal letters, your printed name. Sometimes it's a good idea to include a reference, which may summarise the content: *Repairs to garden tractor*; or identify previous correspondence. Such references are usually underlined and go under the introduction (*Dear Mr Holmes*) and above the first line of the contents.

Now, the planning. This is really another term for thought. In fact, three thoughts:

- Think about the **reason** you're writing the letter. If there are several reasons, separate them clearly and logically in your mind. Put them in order of importance.

- Separate **facts** from your **opinions**. State the facts first, then add your opinions or comments if you must.

- Focus sharply again on your reason for writing. What **result** do you want? What do you want the recipient to do? In an extreme case, what will you do if the recipient doesn't do as you wish?

If you write by hand or use a typewriter, then it pays to do a draft which gives you the opportunity to correct and change and polish the text. Does it make the points clearly? Does it flow? Is every word spelt correctly? (Quick! The dictionary!) As with all writing, try to put yourself in the shoes of the intended reader and imagine the reaction. Is it what you intended? Take your time and get it right.

If you use a word processor, you will be familiar with the 'edit as you go' technique which allows you to make corrections and revisions at will. When you are satisfied with what you see on your screen, then print. Check the printout carefully: it's amazing how many errors you pick up when reading the printed word!

Your final version should be free of errors, well laid out and inviting to read. If you write more than one letter a week (that's 50 a year) it would make sense to have a letterhead printed. A neat letterhead undoubtedly adds a touch a gravitas to any correspondence. Most towns have a franchised fast printing and copying centre that will print a couple of hundred letterheads for you at competitive prices. Or a good wordprocessor will let you create your own, very easily. Alternatively you could have a self-inking name and address stamp made for less than £10. These last several years with normal use and have the added advantage of allowing you to letterhead any size paper and have your name and address on the backs of envelopes.

When addressing an envelope be sure it bears all the information necessary for sure and safe delivery, including the vital postcode. If you are unsure of how to address a person, there's a guide to forms of address later in this book.

Finally, in this chapter on generalised advice:

● When writing business or non-personal letters, be clear and concise.

● In personal correspondence to those you know and love, be yourself (but preferably personable and as informal and honest as you dare!)

The Willows,
26 Long Barn Lane,
Wilmardenden,
Kent CT8 5TW

July 1, 1999

Mr G W Holmes,
Managing Director,
Gnome Garden Engineering Ltd,
Forklift Road,
Romford, Essex RM7 2DY

Dear Mr Holmes,

Begin your letter here. If you don't know who the managing director is you could hazard a 'Dear Sir or Madam'; or, better still, phone the firm's switchboard and ask for the managing director's name and initials.

Indent each subsequent paragraph similar to the first, like this. When you come to the end of your letter, close with either 'Yours sincerely' if you know the recipient, or 'Yours faithfully' if you don't. If you are writing to an official whom you've never met and are not likely to meet, sign off with 'Yours truly'. None of these sign-offs are set in stone, however.

Yours faithfully,
[sign here]
[your name here]

Relationships by post: Strictly Personal

We may be the last generation to write to each other.

Philip Larkin

Personal Letters

Personal correspondence runs parallel to one's life, from birth announcements and thank you notes for christening gifts through love letters, apologies and get well cards to letters of condolence. For all of this you need to cultivate a personal voice in your correspondence: light and friendly, sincere and sympathetic, affectionate and loving, according to the occasion and the recipient.

Personal letters will inevitably convey your thoughts and emotions, but you need to measure your emotions with care. There will be moments in your life when you're tempted to open the floodgates of your heart to a correspondent. Just remember that your outpourings will be on permanent record, which is fine if they remain in safe and discreet hands but emotionally scarring if they don't.

Perhaps the most common of personal communications is the thank you note. As simple a concept as it is, many people, intending to lay on thick slabs of rapturous gratitude, finish up with a terse, flat 'Fred and I wish to thank you for the knitted tea cosy'. Yet gift-givers are almost always so delighted to receive grateful acknowledgements that it's worthwhile honing your thank you skills, and some pointers are given in this chapter.

An oft-heard question is: should a personal note be handwritten? The short answer is yes – if your handwritting is neat enough. Handwritten notes are certainly appreciated. But if your handwriting is semi-legible, typescript is perfectly acceptable.

And it is even more acceptable if the introduction – *Dear John/Judy/Mrs Smith* – and perhaps the close – *Ever yours/With much love,* etc – are handwritten. Because thank you letters are so prized, it's worth remembering that these need not be limited to acknowledging presents and hospitality. If somebody has helped you in some way, and given generously of their time or support, a gracious thank you note is not only likely to be appreciated, but also remembered and treasured.

Monday

My dear Anne,

What a wonderful weekend! Can I hope that you enjoyed it as much as I did? For me it will always remain one of the most deliriously exciting occasions of my life.

The real reason for this letter is to say, once again, that I love you. It gives me a thrill just to write that down. Let me throw caution to the winds – do you love me? I can't tell you how happy I'd be to know that you feel the same way about me as I do about you. All I can say is, I've never felt anything like this before in all my life.

I know it's a big step making such a commitment and I will understand your hesitation. But something tells me, excuse the cliché, that we're made for each other. In just under a week we'll be together again and when you look into my eyes (and my heart) you'll know, you'll really know, that I speak the truth. My beautiful Anne, is it our fate to become the two happiest people in all the world?

I think of you constantly. I love you.

Billy

Love Letters

- Handwritten letters are preferred and advised, as is best quality stationery. In your fervid state, don't forget the postage stamp.

- Don't lapse into mushiness. Be gentle, tender and understanding.

- Don't give the impression that you're doing the object of your desire a great favour. A little humility can work wonders.

- Note the simple, sincere-sounding *I love you* at the end.

May 15

My dearest love,

I know we'll be together on June 5 but I have something I want to say to you that simply won't wait.

To say that my heart is bursting with love for you would be an understatement. Every day away from you is Chinese water torture. But, hell, all that's happening is that my love for you gets stronger, day by day.

Of course I would rather be with you, take your hand in mine, kneel before you and plead with you to marry me. But I'm not with you, hence this letter and this heartfelt plea: my dearest love, will you marry me?

You already know my situation (generous but poor) my ambitions (to reach the sky) and my prospects (fairly reasonable, we'll be millionaires in a few months).

But whatever you think, I know that together we'll make a fantastic team. So please, please, say yes. YES! If you do, my life will be complete, and I know that ours together will be completely happy. So, my love, please write, or phone or send your message with the angels. I wait, but meanwhile I give you all my love, everything,

Greg

Marriage Proposals

- For a letter like this you should be mentally on one knee. Try to put into persuasive words what you'd be saying to her in a real situation.

- Try to achieve a balance of deep sincerity and enthusiasm. Absolutely no doubts.

- Even though it's a momentous, life-changing proposal, don't let your sense of humour desert you.

- Think about the both of you. Don't paint too glowing a future.

Friday

My Darling,

Here's my answer – yes. Yes, YES, YES! Or, for the record, yes, I will marry you. I can't wait to tell you again when we're together next week.

You've made me the happiest woman alive. I dream of you, I daydream about you, I fantasise about our future together and of being with each other for ever and ever.

I never had any doubts, not one. Or perhaps just one – whether I will live up to your belief in me. And to put you at ease, Mum and Dad are thrilled to bits, not only for my happiness but to have you as a son. You know they love you to pieces.

I miss you but I love your letters. You have time to send me another one before next week, so please do. I'm so happy. And I love you more than you know.

Alice

Accepting a Marriage Proposal

- If your feelings are genuine, transmit your enthusiasm to paper and give him a moment to remember all his life.

- Not a bad idea to set him at his ease about the family. Of course if they're a bit anti the young man you'll need to be gentle but realistic: 'You've taken Mum and Dad by surprise and I'm sure you'll understand they'll need a little time. But it won't make any difference to us'. Already the teamwork is in evidence.

- Don't frighten him off with too many wedding details and problems.

January 2

Dear Arnold,

I received your letter this morning and I was stunned and flattered by your proposal and kind remarks about me.

Arnold, you know that I care for you a lot. I admire you, enjoy your company and value your affection and friendship. But I do not love you and I know you will agree with me that without it no relationship like marriage can succeed.

That is why I am deeply sorry to have to tell you that my answer is no. I am certain that my feelings will not change.

I am aware that my refusal will hurt you and that I am in danger of losing your friendship and companionship. Please, I hope not. I also sincerely hope that on reflection you will come to believe this is the best course for both of us.

Let us stay friends. With deep affection,

Gloria

Rejecting a Marriage Proposal

- Keep it short.

- Don't fudge. Make it crystal clear, as gently but as firmly as you can, that the party's over.

- Make absolutely plain that your answer is final and that your feelings and decision won't change. Otherwise matters could drag on and become untidy.

- Let the poor guy retain some dignity by stressing his good qualities and valuing your continued friendship.

May 19

Dear John,

Thank you for the dinner and club last night. I had such a good time and enjoyed your company so much that what I have to say to you now is going to sound ungrateful and contemptible. I beg you, John, it is really not like that.

Although we've been together now for over two years and have had many, many happy times together, I've never thought of our relationship as anything but a very fond friendship. But, by the tone of the letter you wrote recently, and from what you said to me last night, I fear that you think we are much closer.

At the great risk of hurting you I have to be honest and tell you that although I regard you as a dear friend I do not love you. It may have got close to that but deep down I know that, now and in the future, I cannot return your feelings towards me.

It hasn't been easy to write this but I would hate it if you thought I'd been deceiving you. If you can bear it, I still want to see you and hope we can meet again soon.

Until then, affectionately,

Joan

Dear John . . . Dear Joan . . .

- This style of 'Dear John' or rejection letter can double for either a man or a woman.

- If the other partner's gushing love is to be diminished to mere friendship, try to make the lesser relationship sound as attractive a prospect as possible. If, on the other hand it's the end of the line, then draw the line firmly.

- Keep it short, though not brusque, and make your intentions crystal clear.

Monday

Dear Pansy,

I got the news this morning and can't wait to congratulate you and Freddie on your engagement.

Although we have known each other most of our lives I have only known Freddie for the six months since he came into your life. But even in that short time I have come to realise what an ideal couple you make! You must be over the moon, and your parents must be delighted.

Let's meet soon – I want to hear it all. And please give my love and congratulations to Freddie.

Your devoted friend,

Millie

Congratulations on an Engagement/Marriage

- These are among the most pleasant forms of personal correspondence, so don't hold back on your goodwill or enthusiasm.

- A letter like this will help cement your friendship to the couple, who'll value and remember your supportive and affectionate response.

- Letters similar in tone can also be sent to the couple's parents although some might regard this as cynical networking.

June 30

Dear Pat and Don,

I can't tell you how thrilled we were when we unwrapped your most generous gift.

How could you have known that Jamie is a fiend for toast? He almost fainted with joy when he tried out the automatic individual slice popup control. And you chose green! How did you know that will be perfect in our kitchen-to-be?

It was lovely seeing you both at our wedding, and when we settle down (we're temporarily in Jamie's old flat) I'll let you know. Once again, many thanks.

Love,

Margaret

Thanks for the Present

- Undoubtedly over the top but think of the warm glow you'll give the recipients! Although the use of 'Thanks for the Gift' cards is increasing, a personal, preferably handwritten, note wins hands down for sincerity.

- A personal note can soften the rather calculated way in which such gifts are solicited nowadays (tick off the list of suggestions, phone the store, etc).

- Unsolicited gifts from those who were not invited to the wedding deserve a very special letter of thanks.

- In all such letters be sure to acknowledge what the present actually is.

- If the gift is money, the donors might get enjoyment from knowing how you intend to spend or use it.

Sunday

Dear Mrs Morgan,

     It was most thoughtful and kind of you to visit me yesterday.

     Thoughtful, because through a mutual friend you found out that I was rather lonely and feeling sorry for myself, and kind because you took a couple of hours from your very busy schedule to come and see me.

     Your visit cheered me up immensely and you'll be pleased to know that I spent most of this morning in the garden, due to your encouragement.

     You have my heartfelt thanks,

Yours sincerely,

Elizabeth Curzon

Saying Thanks

- Who could fail to be touched and rewarded by the gratitude so sincerely and graciously expressed in a note like this? Handwritten, of course.

- Similar thank you letters (for gifts, visits, hospitality, a timely note of sympathy or support, some special effort) should pay tribute to thoughtfulness, kindness, generosity, forbearance, compassion, solicitude, etc.

- A teacher who'd spent out-of-hours time helping your child, a neighbour who towed your crippled car to a garage, a colleague who took the trouble to check on your family's needs while you were hospitalised – all would be pleased to be thanked but more than pleased to receive a thank you letter.

September 2

Dear Uncle Ernest,

I remember that when you were down here last Christmas you asked me to keep you posted about my new business. You told me then that you thought the 'Ezy Bulb Planter' I was developing should be a big commercial success.

Unfortunately this has turned out not to be the case. The two firms I hired to manufacture the item struck problems and abandoned the project and although contractually I am in the right they cost me nearly £30,000 with nothing to show for it.

As a result I face losing my business and everything I've sunk into it. Ironically I've now found a new manufacturer who's solved the problems, but unless I can find £6,000 within two weeks I will face bankruptcy – at twenty-seven!

You know I've put everything I have, physically, mentally and financially, into the business. I've worked an average 16 hours a day for two years. I've borrowed to the limit (Mum and Dad have helped, of course). Uncle Ernest, it's not easy making this appeal and I apologise unreservedly for writing to you. But you are my last resort, my final hope. If you can manage to lend me the £6,000 you will see every penny back.

I will understand totally if you can't see your way to helping me financially. And regardless of what you decide, I would in any case welcome any advice you can give me.

Your affectionate nephew,

Michael

Saying Please

- The outcome of begging letters is notoriously difficult to predict. Instead of producing the desired effect (money) they can result in misunderstanding, hostility, family quarrels and total estrangement. So beware!

- Give a brief background to the crisis but also stress the positive outcome (if there is one) if £x will solve the problem. A would-be benefactor might consider being a rescuer but balk at throwing good money after bad.

- A flattering end-note (asking for advice) might help hit the right button.

Sunday

My Dear Toby,

We've just heard from your mother about your graduation, and Aunt Josie and I are just as thrilled as she is.

What a wonderful achievement – and you've worked so hard for it, too. We're particularly pleased that you've proved yet again that there are brains in the family!

Obviously we're keen to know about your plans for the future, so make sure you write, and also visit us soon.

Once again, our wholehearted congratulations.

Love from us both,

Albert

Congratulations

- Being offered congratulations is a life-enhancing experience.

- For many people it doesn't happen too often, so when some achievement (graduating, having a baby, getting a first job or a promotion, learning to fly, passing a driving test) is greeted with written congratulations, it can make someone's day.

- Make it short and sweet, on a card if you like, and preferably handwritten.

Stonefield,
Cherrytree Lane,
Marstone, Bath,
BA2 7CV
Day of Atonement

My Dearest Abigail,

How can I apologise for my behaviour at your luncheon party yesterday? Although my recollections are muddled I now realise that I must have upset your guests, embarrassed you and Bill and generally made an obnoxious fool of myself.

It was completely unforgivable, but I hope you will find the generosity to forgive and forget. The thought of losing your friendship over my display of stupidity is more than I can bear. Can I assure you that what happened was untypical and will never, never happen again.

With fond regards to you both,

Ted

Apologies

- A difficult letter to write, and demanding a high order of courage. But should you decide to write an apology, don't hold back. To work it must be an all-out, grovelling, hand-wringing, reproachful confessional.

- Ask for forgiveness and pray that the transgression will be deeply buried and forgotten.

- Write promptly and arrange to see the victims soon to avoid having the incident fester in their minds.

- Don't rely entirely on written words. Accompany them with flowers.

Thursday

Dear Arthur,

      Ellen told me that you were spending your holidays this year at St Catherine's, you lucky thing – warm bed, loads of pretty women eager to do anything for you (anything??), just lying about all day doing nothing – where can I buy a ticket?

      I'm told also that everything went well and that you're doing fine, so keep up the good work. And don't be too impatient – on the outside it's wet and cold and grey and last night Jack was caught in a five-mile motorway tailback due to fog. And my car's in the garage; I spun on the ice last week, hit a brick wall and demolished the front end and lights – such fun!

      Sam also has car troubles – his was stolen and although it was eventually found it was minus the radio and his favourite leather jacket.

      But the good news is that Heather's young man has asked her to marry him (do you remember Trevor? He has an engaging lisp) and I won the bridge prize last week.

      Anyway, Arthur, relax and enjoy your holiday and you'll be well and fit in no time. We think of you all the time.

Love from us all at No.36,

Deborah

Get Well

- When you hear of a friend or colleague in hospital the knee-jerk reaction is to send off one of the thousands of cards published specifically for the occasion. But after a week or two, when the clutter of cards has been cleared from the bedside unit, a letter can be a godsend to a bed-bound patient.

- Avoid dwelling on medical matters, keep it cheerful and pack it with news and gossip that can be recycled during visiting hours.

June 15th

My dear Carol,

We are deeply saddened by your mother's death and our sympathies and condolences go out to you and your family.

Although we hadn't seen your mother during the last few years our memories of her will always remain. She was so big-hearted and generous that just thinking of her gives us a warm glow of deep and lasting affection.

We will miss her terribly but the loss to you must be incalculable.

There must be ways in which we can help you at this most painful time. Lauren will call you next week, and I hope to see you very soon.

You are constantly in our thoughts.

In sorrow and sympathy,

Lauren and Roy Green

Condolences (intimate and informal)

- Avoid cards; write a brief, comforting hand-written note as soon as you can after hearing about the death. Offer help as well as sympathy.

- Write from your heart; feelings honestly expressed, however clumsily, will always be appreciated. But contain your emotions or you risk sounding mawkish.

- Offer a recollection of the deceased if you wish: fond memories a particular occasion, a summary of the person's outstanding qualities.

- Don't dwell on the circumstances surrounding the death; rather try to take the recipient's mind forward – to some future event or meeting.

> 134 Haywood Drive,
> Marling, Nr Picton, Kent
> Tel. 01899 221216
> December 12

Dear Mrs Long,

     I would like to express my sincere condolences to you over your sad loss of Harry.

     You may have difficulty remembering me but I met you on a couple of occasions at Harry's firm's golf days.

     I would like you to know that Harry will always have an important place in my memory. I owe him an enormous debt of gratitude for his unfailing help in my career. He was both wise and generous as I'm sure you know. He also guided me through a distressing and emotional period when I lost my little daughter and, a short while later, when my wife left me.

     Losing Harry is a grievous blow to me, so I know his loss must be overwhelming for you.

     Please accept my deep sympathy and if there is any way in which I can help you, please let me know.

Yours sincerely,

Richard Milton

Condolences (to a non-acquaintance)

- Sending condolences to a relative or close acquaintance can be a matter of duty. Expressing your sympathy to a bereaved person who doesn't or hardly knows you is an act of compelling unselfishness.

- Your duty in such cases is to provide a personal testament to the deceased, simply and sincerely. Coming 'out of the blue' as it were, such letters are invariably valued by the bereaved, and may even offer new insights on the life of the loved one.

Jane Bush,
12 Potsdam Road,
Mercator,
Bolton,
BL2 9QR
01720 045671
June 22

Dear Mr Parish,

Please accept my thanks for your kind letter and your very kind words about Jeremy.

I have been deeply touched by the dozens of letters and cards I've received, and comforted to know how much Jeremy was admired and loved.

Thank you for your thoughts and for your offer to help. It is exceedingly generous of you and I shall certainly contact you should the need arise.

Yours sincerely,

Jane Bush

Responding to Sympathy and Condolences

- Although it is quite common to acknowledge letters of sympathy and condolences with cards, writing a letter, when the emotional landscape has cleared a little, can be cathartic.

- It is an unfortunate fact that after a death many bereaved people find themselves facing an unexpectedly lonely existence. Part of the reason is that friends and acquaintances are sometimes hesitant to make contact, perhaps feeling that they might be intruding on the person's privacy and grief. Writing letters can provide a vital link to continuing relationships.

Sunday

Dear Mick,

I was sorry to hear that you and Margot have decided to separate. I know that you've had your difficulties lately so it wasn't a total surprise; nevertheless I had hoped you would find a way to rediscover your former happiness.

Is there anything I can do to help? As you know I love and care for you both, so it's a double dilemma for me.

Would it help if I spoke to Margot? At the risk of being thought an interfering so-and-so I will do anything I can to help you two back together again. But if it is not to be, then you know you will always have my love and friendship and that you can pick up the phone any time and call –

Your devoted friend,

Judy

Commiseration

- Certain misfortunes can be soul-destroying: separation and divorce, bankruptcy and redundancy; sudden disablement, a shop-lifting or drunk-driving charge . . . personal catastrophes that can wreck the life of a friend, relative or colleague. Do you comfort, or walk away?

- Writing a letter of comfort to someone caught up in a personal tragedy can be like walking over broken emotional glass and is never without its dangers, but knowing that someone cares can help restore that person's shattered self-confidence and hope for the future.

April 14

Dear Arnold,

I'm sorry to have to write this letter but I see no other way of appealing to you to pay back the £400 I lent you last December.

As you know this is not the first time I've asked you for repayment but now I really must have the money as I'm way overdrawn at the bank, all because of that loan. Our agreement, by the way, was that you would repay it all within six weeks. So it's long overdue.

I know you've had problems and from our long acquaintance I know you to be completely honest and a person of integrity, so I have no doubt you will pay me. And if, for any reason you cannot right now, I'm sure you would tell me so that we could work something out.

Arnold, I desperately need that money, and now. It would be crazy if this matter ended a long and enjoyable friendship, wouldn't it? So please call or write urgently.

George

The Gloved Fist

- When a friend or relative won't pay back a loan and goodwill is running low, you want to send out a lynching party, not a letter. But confrontational anger is a last resort and can result in legal action, shattered relationships – and still no money.

- Letters that express your disappointment and anger can be written without intemperate language and wild threats. Make your points firmly, of course, but allow that the misdemeanour is untypical and forgivable.

- Cool reason and an appeal to the person's sense of fairness is more likely to be productive than hostile fireworks.

Saturday

Dear Gran,

I'm sure you know how Bill and I feel about private schools, and although your generosity would otherwise have been appreciated, we do not think it is fair of you to go over our heads as you have been doing.

You have put the children's names down at two schools when there is no chance of their ever going to them. So the result is that it confuses the children, wastes the time of the schools and wastes our time and money – making sure the schools are not misled about our intentions.

We know you worry and care about your grandchildren's future, as do we. But they are our children and we are responsible for their welfare in every way.

The last thing we want is for the children to become victims of a battle between you and us, so could you please drop the private school idea? There is so much else you could do for them – such as a buying them a computer, or paying for music or riding lessons.

Your loving Bill and Delia

Ticking off Granny

- Not all personal and family relationships run smoothly. Occasionally someone will step over the line, requiring a (initially) polite reprimand.

- Usually a face to face discussion is the best way to solve family and personal differences but sometimes this may neither be possible nor – if the perpetrator is inclined to be terminally unreasonable and argumentative – prudent. A letter might achieve the right balance of firmness and persuasion without too much damage to relationships.

Writing to Children

Adults often face difficulties when contemplating a letter to a child: how can I relate to a child's age and interests without writing a lot of embarrassing and mawkish twaddle?

That shouldn't put you off, however. Children today receive so few, if any, letters addressed to them they must wonder what a letter is! So it's worth the effort to introduce a child to the pleasures of intimate correspondence. And who knows – you could receive a letter in return!

Most children are inquisitive, so tell them what you've been doing, where you've been, who you've met (and what you think of them). Ask a lot of questions, too, perhaps about school and friends, Mum and Dad and brothers and sisters. Enclosing a stamped, addressed envelope is a good wheeze to encourage a reply.

Announcements and Invitations

Announcements and invitations hardly aspire to be personal letters, but even these can benefit from a knowledge of the principles of written etiquette. A good many still retain, probably unintentionally, the pomposity of a more formal age, whereas today we generally prefer a more relaxed approach to such correspondence.

There are cards for all occasions, of course, in an almost overwhelming choice.

Beginning at the beginning, with births, the news of the happy arrival is usually spread via a card, the appropriate columns of the local newspaper, or by word of mouth.

There isn't a lot to say about a baby other than that it has arrived and that it is a boy or a girl with such and such a name, so to announce it with a letter seems excessive.

More appropriate to a letter is the christening:

---

                                    12 Abbot's Parkway,
                                    Arnott's Grove, Belford
                                    Notts NG4 TH8

Dear Margaret and Toby,

Holly Mae will be christened on Sunday, June 4, at St Stephen's Church, Centre Street, Tonborough.

The service will begin at 4pm but before then we are having drinks at home from 2.30 and we would love you to be there.

After the service you are also welcome to return here for further celebrations!

Love, Joan and Ken

Although many people like copperplate formality for parties and receptions, others prefer a lighter, more informal touch for their invitations. Whatever the tone, though, don't forget the essential information.

Bowing to tradition and convention, wedding announcements invariably take on a formal tone and appearance – almost always in the form of an elegantly printed card. Bucking the custom with something more original and cheerful could mean a lighter, less formal touch. Remember, however, that this is the bride's (or her parents) department. The usual formula is:

Lucinda and Geoffrey Barnes
would be delighted if you could join them
to celebrate the engagement of their daughter
Pauline
at a party in the Admiralty Room, Nelson Hotel,
Wharf Crescent, Port Abington,
on Saturday, September 20, at 8.00pm.

RSVP   Party frocks
'The Grove', Elm Tree Drive   Lounge suits
Abington (01447) 320 432

The invitation has a similar style:

Mr and Mrs Hugh Blake
request the pleasure of the company of

_____

at the marriage of their daughter Susan Emily
to Mr James McNicholl
at St Swithin's Church, Normanville
on Saturday, May 3, at 3 o'clock

An RSVP should be appended to the invitation or, more thoughtfully, an addressed reply card could be included for the guest's response.

When replying to invitations, a good rule is to match the style of your reply to that of the invitation. If handwritten, it is a courtesy to reply similarly; on the other hand a formal invitation suggests a formal reply. While that's straightforward enough some people have a problem finding the words to gracefully decline an invitation.

There are two things to remember: be complimentary, disappointed and apolgetic, and explain the reasons for your inability to attend:

March 6

Dear Lynne and Charles,

We're distraught! We were delighted to get your kind invitation until we checked the family diary and were dismayed to find that we have a long-standing engagement to spend the day with June's parents in Norwich that weekend. We only visit them a couple of times a year so we can't let them down. It's a great shame.

So please accept our apologies – and our best wishes for a great party!

Yours in tears,

Jack and Bernice

Of all announcements, a letter advising relatives and friends of a death is the saddest and probably the most difficult to write. Unsurprisingly many bereaved people prefer to send out a simple, formal card, or use the telephone, not least because the days surrounding a death are confused and chaotic. However there may be circumstances that require a personal letter to convey the news with greater sensitivity. This solemn duty may, if you are a close relative or friend of the deceased, fall to you.

August 10

Dear Mr and Mrs Howard,

It is my sad duty to inform you that Mary's mother died yesterday, August 9.

Her life ended painlessly and peacefully after her long illness.

Mary has asked me to thank you both for your devotion to her mother and for your many visits and gifts, which Ellen always looked forward to with eager delight.

Ellen's funeral will take place at the East Chapel, Fulham Crematorium, at 11 am, Friday, August 13.

Yours sincerely,

Adam Santangelo

Protecting your interests: Complaining with Effect

Caveat emptor – Let the buyer beware.

Even the most careful consumer occasionally gets lumbered with a defective appliance, a bodged plumbing job, a phantom delivery, an inaccurate bank statement.

In the great majority of cases the supplier is only too happy to set things right. But there are always the sloppy, intransigent or plain crooked traders who'll evade their responsibilities, and they can make your life hell. If you let them.

Knowing how to complain effectively when you're a victimised consumer is one of life's essential arts. Knowing who to complain to is also important.

First in your sights should be the person or firm who actually sold you the faulty goods or services. It is worth remembering that if you have paid with cash or by credit card, your claim is not against the manufacturer, importer or wholesaler, but the retailer or seller. If you used a credit card you are further protected by the Consumer Credit Act which makes the credit card company responsible.

A further line of defence is the Sale and Supply of Goods Act which stipulates that goods or services must be 'as described', must be of good quality and work satisfactorily, and must be fit for the purpose for which they are sold. The seller or supplier is legally bound to make sure that all of these apply; if not, you must be compensated.

Other legislation that protects your interests includes the Consumer Protection Act, which prohibits labels or advertisements with misleading prices; the Trade Descriptions Act, which forbids traders to make false claims about the goods or services they sell; the Unfair Contract Terms Act, which protects purchasers' rights from the 'small print' in contracts; and the Food Safety Act which protects consumers from unsafe or sub-standard foodstuffs.

If you fail to get redress, you can turn to various consumer watchdogs, including municipal advice bureaux, regional Departments of Fair Trading, the

Department of Trading Standards, a number of trade regulatory authorities, ombudsmen – all of which you can get from your nearest Citizen's Advice Bureau. Finally, you can consult your local MP or a solicitor.

But first, the letter. It is absolutely vital to keep and copy all receipts, documents and relevant correspondence. However aggrieved you may feel, don't begin your complaint by antagonising the supplier. State the facts clearly and concisely. Make it clear what it is you want: a replacement, a refund, a repair or compensation. Keep cool and calm, and you'll collect.

You may find that your first letter fails to achieve the desired response. Try again. Perhaps it didn't make your case strongly enough, or it was read by the wrong person.

Maybe it found its way on to the 'too hard' pile. More likely, you were being fobbed off: 'Sorry, your complaint should have been made within 30 days . . . it is our policy not to make refunds . . . we do not guarantee that product . . . it's the manufacturer's problem, not ours.' None of these responses is legally valid, so try again. This time, get some advice and quote the relevant Act so that they know they're not dealing with an innocent.

In the following pages, you'll find suggested letter formats designed to deal with some of the more common areas of complaint. It would be rare for two causes of complaint to be exactly the same, so each must be adapted to the circumstances.

But before getting down to details, here are some tips:

- If you've been unable to get anywhere by complaining in person or over the telephone, a letter backed by solid facts is hard to ignore.

- Rather than address your letter to some anonymous executive, call the firm's switchboard and ask for the name of, say, the general manager, sales manager or marketing director. In larger firms, senior management may be surprised to learn that their company is treating its customers unfairly.

- Don't attach original receipts or documents to your letter – always use copies. Originals can sometimes get 'lost'.

- Don't threaten legal action in your initial correspondence; it is always taken with a grain of salt. Save it for a final showdown.

- If you are forced, at last, into taking legal action, either use a solicitor or make sure you know the working of the procedures of Small Claims Courts (for amounts under £5,000 in England and Wales; £750 in Scotland; £1,000 in Northern Ireland). Apply directly to the courts for advice and information.

Monday, May 12

Dear Mr O'Brien,

Every day and evening during the past week (May 4-11) we have been disturbed by excessive noise from your garage adjoining this house. The noise is, I understand, due to your automotive engine tuning business.

On three occasions I have asked you to eliminate or reduce the noise to an acceptable level but it has continued unabated. I have explained to you that the noise is distressing and is affecting our health. Mrs Burns has suffered almost continual headaches during this past week.

I am therefore forced to give you notice that if the nuisance continues beyond today I will instruct my solicitor to initiate legal proceedings against you, including a restraining order and a claim for compensation.

Yours faithfully,

Gordon H Burns

Fighting Environmental Pollution

- Installing proper sound reduction baffles is going to cost Mr O'Brien a packet, so don't expect him to give in easily. But give in he must, because today noise pollution is widely recognised as one of the main environmental actors that can make people's lives a misery.

- When appeals and warnings have gone unheeded, a no-nonsense letter is called for – one that makes the consequences clear. But you must be prepared to carry out your threat, or any future warnings and letters will ring hollow – the worst noise of all.

32 Assize Court,
Permberton Road, Glaston,
Mouton, Exeter EX2 4NG
December 9

Planning Officer,
Highways Department,
Exeter City Council,
42 High St, Exeter EX1 2CE.

Dear Sir,

The paving outside the above address and along Pemberton Road is broken and dangerous. I have stumbled on it several times and at least one other resident, an old lady, is afraid to risk walking on the pavement for fear of an accident.
Will you please have the paving repaired, urgently.

Yours faithfully,

R J Thomas

Writing to the Council

- As above, keep it simple, factual and unemotional, no matter how many times you've twisted your ankle. Councils know by now that they are liable for compensation if you have an accident attributable to their lack of maintenance and care, so a letter like this will get action.

- Make a phone call to find out to whom you should be writing, and get a name. If you don't, your letter could ricochet around the corridors of local power for months.

Mrs A W Wilson,   October 2
Tour Booking Director,
Sunset Holidays,
High Street, Bath.

Dear Mrs Wilson,

     I wish to make a complaint about the holiday I booked at your office on July 19 this year (Ref: MAJ20232677).

     Your booking assistant confirmed then that we would have a large, air-conditioned double room with a spacious balcony directly overlooking the beach. The en-suite bathroom was to have both a shower and bath. We also chose the 'A' class accomodation because it gave us access to the garden pool.

     Instead, what we got was a cramped room without air-conditioning. The bathroom had no bath. The balcony overlooked a drab apartment block with washing lines. The beach and sea were not to be seen. The garden pool was empty.

     I pointed all this out to your courier Mr Sanchez, who was sympathetic but could do nothing. Our annual holiday was completely spoiled.

     Quite clearly your firm failed to discharge its contractural and legal obligations and this letter is to inform you that I hold you liable for our failed holiday and that I am seeking compensation. Please let me have your proposals for compensation within seven days.

Yours faithfully,

G N Hampton

Holiday Woes

- Complaints about miserable holidays are unfortunately fairly routine and many operators have a fairly slick routine to deflect or minimise them. So it is important to be specific: set out exactly what you were promised, and what was really delivered, but keep in mind that most holiday brochures come laden with hectares of fine print.
[See following letter]

Tour Booking Director,
Sunset Holidays Ltd,
High Street, Bath BA3 4YW

July 14

Dear Sir/Madam,

Your Ref: CR2A11568

This will confirm that I have booked the 10-day Tuscan Holiday (Ref as above) with you, departing Gatwick August 18 and returning August 28, for which I have paid £740 for two adults including all supplements.

Please note that I have also booked the following special requirements:

(1) Spacious second-floor room with double bed and en-suite bathroom with uninterrupted landscape views;

(2) baby cot suitable for 2-year old child.

If for any reason you cannot confirm any of the above please advise me immediately.

Yours faithfully,

(Mrs) Joyce Mitchell

Confirming Holiday Arrangements

- An increasing number of holiday makers are ensuring that any special requirements agreed upon when making the booking are confirmed by both parties before departure.

- Although this procedure won't guarantee that things won't go wrong, it should certainly make everything easier if you have to complain when you return.

- If this safeguard fails to protect you and your letters seeking compensation are ignored or disputed, you should write to the Association of British Travel Agents (ABTA), 55 Newman Street, London W1P 4AH.

10 Arcadia Lane
Bushampton,
Kilmarnock KA6 4BV

The Manager,
Historic Art & Artifacts Ltd,
Brayville Road,
Edinburgh EH14 8NY

Order No. HAA2356

Dear Sir/Madam,

I wish to complain about the delivery of the pair of Clarice Cliff brooches (Cat. No. 2136, £47.50 plus £2.95 postage) I ordered on December 2 but which did not arrive until Christmas Eve, December 24.

Your catalogue clearly stated that Christmas orders placed before December 5 would be guaranteed delivery in the UK within 14 days. Thus my order should have been delivered by December 16 at the latest. The brooches were intended as a Christmas gift to a friend in Germany but they arrived far too late to be forwarded in time. Instead I had to buy an alternative gift.

I am deeply disappointed. The items are enclosed and I request a full and prompt refund (£47.50 plus £2.95 postage plus my return postage).

Yours faithfully,

(Miss) Josephine Barber

Late or Non-Delivery

- The Sale of Goods Act requires suppliers to deliver ordered goods 'within a reasonable time'. The period is rather arbitrary but any delivery taking longer than 28 days should be challenged. In the case above the supplier is definitely in breach of the Act.

- It is important that you act promptly and supply all the relevant order and delivery documentation.

- NB: If it is a damaged or faulty mail order item, the carriage for its return should also be paid by the supplier. Quite often they will send you a pre-paid postage label, or arrange for a carrier to collect it.

26 Afton Way
Banferrie,
Belfast, NI.
September 12

The Manager,
Mercury Motors Ltd,
Market Estate,
Lisburn.

RE: RU7 8HJ

Dear Sir,

On August 30 I purchased an A4 Avant 1.9TDi 210SE red Audi from you. Within three days it developed a serious gear-change problem and severe squealing from the steering mechanism. It is obvious that the car was defective at the time of purchase.

Under the sales agreement you are clearly in breach of contract and bound to make whatever repairs or replacements as are necessary, free of charge. If these take longer than 24 hours I will require a courtesy car during the repair period.

I will call you tomorrow to arrange for the car to be restored to 100% as new roadworthy condition. I reserve my rights under the amended Sale of Goods Act 1979.

Yours faithfully,

Michael Singer

Buying a Lemon

- Buying a lemon when acquiring a car is every driver's nightmare. Heaven forbid if you are caught up in an ill-starred transaction but if you are a blunt letter like the above should help put the calamity on a businesslike basis.

- Despite guarantees there is no guarantee that any amount of repair work and replacements will restore the machine to the car it should have been. That's why it's important to always reserve your rights under the amended Sale of Goods Act which enables you to claim compensation if the repairs prove to be faulty or ineffectual.

56 Zurich Place,
Athelstone Park, Nr Tonbridge,
Kent TN3 6HY
October 13

Service Manager
Overway Motor Services Ltd
Dale St, Tonbridge

Dear Sir,

On October 5 you serviced my Mercedes Estate 230SE, Reg. GKT 984. After driving it home I noticed the automatic steering was unusually stiff and the wheels very difficult to turn. When I asked my local garage what they thought was wrong they found that the steering fluid reservoir had been topped up with gear box oil. This, they said, would severely damage many automatic steering components. It has rendered the car impossible to drive safely.

You have obviously failed to service my car to the standards required by the Supply of Goods and Services Act, under which I am entitled to compensation for breach of contract.

You can either undertake to repair and restore the car to its previous condition, or I will have it done elsewhere and send you the bill. I await your prompt response.

Yours Faithfully,

A T Michaels

Faulty Car Repairs and Servicing

- Next to buying a faulty car, faulty auto repairs produce a veritable hors concours of classic complaints. But you can seek protection under the Supply of Goods and Services Act 1982 which requires contracted work to be carried out with 'reasonable skill and care'.

- Most problems of this kind are dealt with in person or over the phone. But the writer probably forsees trouble ahead, hence the precautionary letter.

DUNTREE COTTAGE,
Fourbush Lane, Allandale
Notts. NG7 4PR
September 19

Mr Peter Price-Williams,
Goulez & Spindler,
Financial Consultants,
Headway House,
Nottingham NG1 8BU   Biltmore Pension 96/665/GS2001

Dear Sir,

About three years ago (23/7/96) I asked you to recommend a pension plan suitable for my retirement at 60, on a monthly budget of £120. In the event you recommended that I transfer my current pension plan into a 20-year Biltmore Personal Insurance plan towards which I have been paying £113 per month.

My accountant has just analysed my current outlay with the expected return and finds that if I had stayed with my former plan I would enjoy the same or better pension benefits on retirement yet I would be paying only £72 per month. This means that I am needlessly paying nearly £10,000 more for my pension. In recommending the above product you have given me bad advice which will leave me severely out of pocket. My accountant estimates my loss to be £9,456.00 over the 20-year period.

As you know you are bound by the Financial Services Act 1986 to deal promptly with my complaint and offer appropriate compensation. I expect your reply within 14 days and, if not forthcoming, I will forward my complaint to the relevant authorities.

Yours,

Bill Forbes

Bad Pension and Financial Advice

- Financial advisors aren't infallible and it is always wise to get a second opinion. If you suspect that the advice you've been given has been over-optimistic or appears to involve you in loss, arrange to meet the adviser and ask for an explanation

- If not satisfied, write a letter demanding restitution which, if your complaint is justified, should lead to negotiations for compensation. Remember that your adviser is regulated by the Personal Investment Authority to whom you should apply if your complaint remains unresolved.

March 15

Apartment 4B,
The Boltons
12 Moulding Road
Brigton, Oxford OX5 6NU

The Manager,
Cafe État Nauseeux ,
Holland Drive, Oxford

Dear Sir,

Last Friday evening I booked a table for four at your restaurant. The table was for 8.00pm. Although we were punctual and ordered our meal promptly the starter course wasn't served until 9.10pm.

The main course arrived at 9.50pm. Two of my guests were served dishes that were a disgrace – a warm crab salad that was decidedly 'off', and aromatic crispy duck which was dry, tough and cold.

I complained immediately to the head waiter who offered to replace the dishes but as this would obviously take some time and it was already late, we declined. The waiter then insisted I would have to pay the entire bill, including the obligatory 15% service!

You managed to ruin our evening out and the least you can do is to refund the cost of the main meals (the other two main courses remained untouched because of the ruckus) plus the service charge – by your menu, £58.50. If I do not receive your cheque for this amount within 14 days I will have a County Court summons served on you for its recovery. You will, of course, be welcome to the free publicity.

Yours faithfully,

Howard J Williams

Rebuking a Restaurant

- When the table you booked has been given away, or you've been served a rotten meal or suffered poor service or been overcharged, complain immediately and try to negotiate some form of compensation.

- If unsuccessful resort to a letter demanding redress, quoting the Consumer Protection Act 1987, The Food Act 1990, or threatening a Small Claims Court summons.

Jane Saunders,
45 Hay Farm Rd,
Cardling,
Bristol BS8 2GJ
August 26

The Manager,
Consumer Bank Ltd,
114 Portside Street,
Bristol BS1 4QP

Dear Sir,

Last month at your suggestion I transferred £600 from my current account into a 'Golden Key' 30-day account as it pays an extra 1% interest.

On my first statement I note that you have charged me £16 for the transfer. No mention was made of this charge at the time, so I would like an explanation.

I also note that your monthly fee for July on my current account was increased from the usual £8 per month to £22, even though the account has always been in credit. Please explain this.

Yours,

Jane Saunders

Querying a Bank Statement

- It may seem laughable but many people go through life believing their bank to be infallible. Not so. Anyone who fails to closely examine their bank statements deserves to lose money from a bank account, not make it.

- In the recent years of intense competition, banks have introduced all kinds of charges, fees and penalties to maximise revenues, so beware.

- That cynical appraisal aside, banks are usually only too ready to put things right if a mistake has been made – but only if you complain.

12 Parkway Close,
Helmsdale,
Worcester WR5 2KM
September 30

Mr Bert Jordan,
Jordan, Tanner & Co,
Apple Ind. Estate,
Mordern, Worcs.

Dear Mr Jordan,

I wish to complain about the extension and other work you carried out at my house at the above address during July.

I am sorry to say that some of the work is of an unsatisfactory standard, which has led to serious defects in the walls (damp patches); the plumbing (leaking radiator) and floor (bad squeaking). A detailed list of these faults is attached.

I must request that you rectify these faults as soon as possible as we cannot use the extension in its present condition.

Yours faithfully,

Edward Byrnes

Defective Building Work

- This letter underlines the importance of having a firm, detailed estimate, counter-signed by both parties, before work commences. This will be of enormous value should there be a dispute later.

- Payment arrangements should also be agreed at this time: how much up front, progress payments, and, most important of all, the sum to be held over for a period (1-3 months is common) to ensure that the builder will make good any defects.

Apt 14F,
Juillard Mansions,
44 Tanner Rd,
Bexton,
York
June 12

Telford Construction Co,
Railway Yards,
23 Beatty Road, York.

Dear Mr Knight,

Thank you for the work you recently completed in our flat, and also for keeping to the fairly demanding timetable. However, I was shocked to note that your final invoice for the work is almost £1,500 more than you quoted. I accept that you found more rot in the floors than you anticipated and had to instal a larger load-bearing beam, but you quoted a fixed price for the work and that constitutes our contract. Your quote made no mention of allowances for any extra work.

I therefore enclose my cheque for the balance of the original quoted amount.

Yours sincerely,

Alan G Glover

Disputing a Builder's Bill

- A common situation: a builder, having quoted a fixed price without reservations, is involved in extra time or expense during the work. Not surprisingly he tries to claw it back from the client. But for all the client knows, such contingencies could (and should) have been included in the quote anyway.

- So you are wise to resist such try-ons and unless you agreed during the progress of the work to pay extra amounts, pay only the sum set out in the original contract.

18 Fosdike Drive,
Llandudno LL4 2BY
November 7

Mrs M Comstock,
Way, Perry & Bond,
126 High Street,
Llandudno LL2 2SX

Dear Mrs Comstock,

I have just received your invoice for commission for introducing a potential buyer for Berry's Farm, Llanrhos.

I called you on November 2 and subsequently confirmed by letter that I had found a buyer for the property myself and requested you to remove it from your books.

Although you introduced a potential buyer who you claim was able and willing to complete the sale, this did not take place. As our agreement stipulated that commission would be paid only if the sale was completed you are therefore not entitled to be paid any commission.

Yours faithfullt,

Amos Watson

Commission Confusion in Real Estate

- Fortunately for the writer of this letter his agreement with the estate agent was 'no sale, no fee', otherwise he would have been required to pay commission because the agent had introduced a buyer who was 'ready, willing and able' to complete the transaction – a claim difficult to disprove.

- Before signing an agent's selling contract be clear on whether it will be a sole, joint or multiple agency, and agree on the scale of commission and the cost (if any) of specific agency services to be provided: advertising, photography, brochures, etc.

'Witherdale'
Church Lane,
Myrecroft,
Peterborough,
PE3 5AY
March 8

The Manager
Consumer Service Division,
SouthElec,
12 Oswald Way, Peterborough.

Dear Sir/Madam,

Ref: A/c No. A8923/0049

I wish to query my last two accounts for electricity used between October 1 and February 28.

The amounts shown on the invoices are higher than usual, despite this house being empty from December 15 to January 28, when all power was shut off.

It would seem that the meter is faulty, or there is an electricity leakage of some kind. Would you be good enough to have the meter tested so that the charges can be adjusted?

Thank you,

(Mrs) Tessa Bayliss

Querying Electricity, Gas, Water and Phone Bills

- If you think you are being overcharged or paying for electricity, gas, water or telephone services you haven't used, phone first to find out to whom in the company you should complain, then write.

- If you have a suspected faulty meter, you may be required to pay for a test, usually refunded if the meter is proved to be defective. If it is you can have your bill reduced, or compensation paid. For all the utility services there are scales of compensation payments made for interrupted supply. If the company is tardy dealing with your complaint, your nearest Citizens Advice Bureau will point you in the direction of the appropriate watchdog.

42A Roper Road
Folly Lake Estate,
Newport NP12 5AR

August 15
Credit Manager,
Newmarket Securities Ltd,
Field House, Newport.

Dear Sir/Madam,

On July 2 last year I purchased an Escoma 75 Multimedia
Computer (Invoice DX23-7561; Credit Agreement NS/DX 7561-96934)
on a hire-purchase agreement with Newmarket Securities Ltd from
Computer Supermarket, Wharf St, Newport.

Since then the computer has developed serious faults which,
despite several service calls, have not or cannot be rectified. The machine
does not function as it should and I now wish to return it and have all my
instalments refunded in full, a total to date of £456 plus service charges of
£72.45. I give notice that no further instalments will be paid.

I understand that my rights in this matter are protected by the
1973 Supply of Goods (Implied Terms) Act, under which I terminate my
hire-purchase agreement with you on the grounds stated above.

Yours faithfully,

Harold J Shields

Terminating a Hire-Purchase Agreement

- Getting goods replaced or your money back from a finance or hire-
purchase company can be a messy business. However you are protected
from faulty or misdescribed goods by the Supply of Goods (Implied
Terms) Act 1973.

- Remember that when you buy something on a hire-purchase
agreement, your contract passes from the seller to the finance or
lending company.

22 Wakefield Drive,
Hazel Park,
Lawen,
Glasgow G17 6TN
December 14

The Manager,
Hilltower Building Society,
Suchard St, Glasgow

Dear Sir,

Account 0214572

I note from my latest statement (Sheet 223) that the monthly Direct Debit payment to Marlborough Technics has increased from £21.80 to £23.

I authorised no such increase and therefore request that (1) you supply an explanation for the change and (2) reinstate the monthly payment to £21.80.

Yours sincerely,

James Speakman

Direct Debits and Standing Orders

- This letter will get a result but unfortunately not the one the writer might expect. Perhaps the writer thought he'd arranged to pay the monthly amount by Standing Order, an arrangement by which the account holder instructs the bank to pay a certain amount at specific intervals. Only the account holder can alter this arrangement.

- With a Direct Debit, however, the account holder makes an agreement with the payee and authorises the bank to pay those amounts requested by the payee. As you can see, the payee may vary these amounts without seeking permission from the account holder.

- If the DD agreement is abused, however, the account holder can claim reimbursement from the bank.

12 Abbott Lane,
Purcell Park,
Perth, PH2 6TG
March 18

Sales Manager,
Trent Glazing Services,
146 Main Terrace,
Perth PH1 7CM

Dear Sir/Madam,

Two days ago, on March 16, I signed a contract for your firm to double-glaze four windows of my house for a sum of £1,230. Since then I have decided that I do not want the work done and wish to cancel the contract.

I was originally called by your firm and told that my house qualified as a "show home" in this district and that half the work would be done free. When I agreed to discuss this I did not realise a salesman would call. As a result I found myself signing a contract for work costing the same as it would have with any other firm. This was not what was originally discussed.

This letter is a formal notice to cancel the contract I signed within the 7-day cooling-off period provided by the Consumer Protection (Cancellation of Contracts Concluded away from Business Premises) Regulations 1987. Accordingly I request the prompt return of the £230 deposit I paid.

Yours faithfully,

(Mrs) Mona Anderson

Cancelling a 'Signed-at-Home' Contract

- The provisions of the 1987 Consumer Protection Regulations has saved tens of thousands of householders kissing goodbye to money committed by contract in a moment of weakness or under pressure from salesmen.

- To qualify for this protection, however, you must not have invited the salesman to your home. In the case above the householder did not realise that she had agreed to have a salesman call and should therefore benefit from the 7-day cooling-off period.

- Be sure to send the letter by Recorded Mail with Proof of Delivery.

76 Egerton Street,
Tranmore,
Telford TF5 8RR
August 23

Hilton Credit & Investment Ltd,
Harboard House, Brass Street,
Birmingham, B16 3ER
Account HCI/247/E880B

Dear Sirs,

On 16 March 1998 I signed the above hire purchase agreement to help me purchase a camper van. Since then I have met the monthly payments of £196.50 on time and expected to do so for the remainder of the 3-year agreement.

Unfortunately owing to an unforseen financial problem, and my wife being declared redundant last week, I will be unable to meet the repayments in full, at least for the time being. I must stress that I have no intention of defaulting on the debt but I must ask you to consider reducing the monthly amounts over a longer repayment period.

I sincerely hope you will consider this request favourably and look forward to discussing revised terms with you.

Yours faithfully,

Andrew Wyatt-Smith

Please Sirs, I can't pay . . .

- Although credit companies prefer clients to pay their hire-purchase commitments in full and on time, they also welcome honesty from debtors who find they can't keep up payments. If you're caught in a payment trap be cooperative and make whatever offer you can reasonably afford.

79 Ivorsen Crescent,
Renfree Park,
Blackpool FY5 8BK
January 4

Claims Division,
Century Insurance Co, Chronicle Buildings,
Gate St, Manchester M2 4BW

Dear Sirs,

Policy No. CI/10041/C887C

I refer you to our previous correspondence regarding my claim on the above policy. In your latest letter you advise that your offer of £3,400 will not be increased, despite my submitting to you an independent loss assessor's estimate of £4,850 for the damage.

Unless I receive a more realistic offer from you within 14 days I regret to advise that our correspondence will be forwarded to the Insurance Ombudsman Bureau, of which you are a signatory, for arbitration.

Yours faithfully,

Guy Robertson, MD

Disputed Insurance Claim: the Last Resort

- There are occasions when an insurance company and a policy holder fail to see eye to eye. If you feel the company's offer (or perhaps non-offer if it argues that damage or loss is not covered by a policy) isn't fair you can pay for an independent assessment, which may help your case.

- If not, you can, as a last resort, appeal to the Insurance Ombudsman Bureau in London. This won't help you, though, if your insurer isn't a signatory to the scheme, so it pays to check on this before you sign any insurance policy.

24 Virginia Street,
Motherwell,
ML15 4DV
December 19

Mr Derek N Baines,
42 Chalker Avenue,
Motherwell ML8 5GB

Re: Accident on North Parade

Dear Mr Baines,

On November 12 an accident on North Parade involving your Ford van G25 RSB resulted in considerable damage to my Volvo Estate P24 GBM.

I have claimed for the damage covered by my comprehensive insurance policy but this still leaves me liable for £640 not covered by the policy, namely for the insurance excess amount, loss of no-claim bonus, a day off work and transport incurred while the car was being repaired.

You have admitted that the accident was caused solely by your negligence and so far I have heard nothing from you or your insurers. As you are legally responsible for the £640 I look forward to receiving this amount. If I do not receive it within 14 days a county court summons will be issued against you.

Yours faithfully,

Arthur Ableman

Claiming Uninsured Expenses from a Negligent Driver

- Claiming on car insurance policies is a complex business, mostly achieved by a plethora of form-filling. But there often remains the even more complex business of claiming compensation for uninsured expenses from a negligent driver or the driver's insurance company (if he iscomprehensively covered).

- This can require considerable patience and persuasion and you may well be driven to recover your loss through a small claims court.

Mr Bertram Clifford,   October 14
Wrangle, Tryon & Clifford,
Solicitors,
22 Beecham Chambers,
Old Road, Belfast BT6 5JK

Dear Mr Clifford,

                    Your Ref: 98/Best vs Gruner/078002

        While I appreciate your firm's work on my behalf in the above
action I feel bound to question your charges as shown on your invoice of
7/10/98.

        While I fully understand that estimates for legal work can never
be precise, your final account is almost double the £2,020 estimate you
gave me on 16/6/98.

        Would you please supply me with a detailed itemization of the
charges?

Yours sincerely,

Anthony G Best

Querying a Solicitor's Bill

- This firm of solicitors is bound by the Solicitors Act 1974 (Section 64)
  to supply the information requested.

- Complaints about alleged overcharging by legal firms is common
  enough although in many cases unjustified. Nevertheless it pays to
  query charges for legal work and also for what you feel is
  incompetent work and undue delay. If you fail to get satisfaction you
  have recourse to a battery of complaint and reassessment bodies,
  beginning with the Law Society.

Avery Crombie & Partners, Architects,
Broadman Place,
Carlisle CA2 3TU
18 February

D P Crombie, Man Dir
Mr Gene McIvor,
Ackerman Publishing Ltd,
27 Parkway, Dundee DD5 4NN

Dear Mr McIvor,

It has come to our notice that in the December issue of your newsletter Fabrication & Construction Calendar, in an article entitled 'Architects on the Take', you referred to this firm as 'one of the most rapacious in the Northern architectural community' and that 'Avery Crombie & Partners benefited from a non-returnable fee arrangement to the tune of over £150,000'.

Both statements are untrue and completely without foundation, libellous, and seriously damaging to the reputation of this firm, to its profitability and to the livelihoods of its employees.

We therefore request that you immediately send to our solicitors, Lawnside & Partners, a letter of retraction to be approved by them and to be published in the five leading fabrication and construction trade journals at your expense; and to be published prominently in the next issue of your Newsletter.

The alternative is swift and unconditional legal action to retrieve our good reputation and to seek substantial damages.

Yours faithfully,

David P Crombie, Man. Dir

Threatening Legal Action

- Letters containing the threat of legal action for non-compliance must be just that: threatening, unequivocal, and with clear demands. The reader must be left in no doubt that you mean business and mentioning the name of your lawyers will help give sharp legal teeth to your threat. Remember: this is a once-only or final shot that might save you from entering the potentially expensive portals of the law courts.

27 Sandy Lane,
Towbridge,
Kent TN1 2CD

Mr Paul Madeson,
Green Landscapes
Robinia Lane, Letram,
Kent TN10 4RF

July 22

Dear Sir,

  I have received your letter of July 15 threatening me with legal action for non-payment of your invoice for £142.50.

  As I have already stated (my letter of June 30) I deducted that amount from your original invoice for landscaping because (a) untreated timber in the pergola had to be replaced and (b) I had to pay an extra £50 in labour costs for the reconstruction. The amount deducted was entirely due to your negligence.

  There is no question of my paying the £142.50. However, to bring this matter to a close and without prejudice, I will offer you a final payment of £50. If this is not acceptable to you please address all future correspondence to my solicitor, Miss J Barnes, 78 Horsefield Rd, Tonbridge TN2 8BC.

Yours faithfully,

John P Rutger

Avoiding Legal Action

- Whatever the merits of your case it is always worthwhile (and usually cheaper in the end) to avoid legal proceedings. Winning in the courts is no guarantee of winning financially as costs can be awarded against both sides.

- If reasoning fails, bury your pride and consider making a compromise offer.

- To protect your right to withdraw or change your offer, insert the words 'without prejudice' which helps to keep your legal options open.

- Directing future correspondence to a solicitor is usually an effective ploy to make your correspondent think twice about taking legal action.

Clerk of the Justices,   May 30
Fixed Penalty Office,
Magistrates' Court,
Maidstone, Kent ME15 6LF

Dear Sir/Madam,

I enclose a parking ticket which I believe should not have been issued to me. The ticket was put on my car, in my presence, at the corner of Taylor and Brown Streets, Maidstone, on Friday Oct 7 at 10.05am.

At the time, as I explained to the parking warden, my car had broken down and I was waiting for assistance.

I would like to contest this case in court but cannot afford the time to do so. However I hope you will agree that, in the circumstances, the ticket was unfairly issued and should be cancelled.

Yours sincerely,

Ian B Scott

Appealing Against a Parking Fine

- If you feel you've been unfairly dealt with by a parking warden (and who doesn't?) and believe you have a good case, it's always worth appealing to the magistrates' court named on the ticket, citing the circumstances.

- In the case above, 'waiting for assistance because of a breakdown' is an excuse as old as the woolsack. It would need to be proven by the attachment of a call-out docket by the AA, RAC or similar organisation.

The Old Forge,
22A Trafford Close,
Amitree, Taunton TA9 4FG
September 2

Director of Planning,
Taunton City Council,
Military Rd, Taunton TA3 2LP

Dear Sir,

Re: Planning Application TC/98/0481/JAV

I wish to object to the planning application submitted by Betmark Meat Products Ltd for the extension of the Bacon Factory at Trafford Field, Amitree.

My primary objection is that the two-storey extension will overlook my conservatory and garden, and for most of every afternoon block off a considerable amount of sunlight. My more comprehensive objections, in greater detail, are attached.

I have viewed the plans and am implacably opposed to the application, which is a gross and unwarrented intrusion on my family's privacy and damaging to our quality of life.

I trust that you and your Planning Commitee will reject this most ill-considered and insensitive application.

Yours sincerely,

Gerald and Frances Holloway

Objecting to a Planning Permission Application

- Applications for planning permission to build homes, factories, barns, extensions or to make any significant changes to the environment have to jump a series of regulatory hurdles. If you are an objector it's your job to make the hurdles as high and unjumpable as you can.

- Keep your objections factual and follow the guidelines for objecting laid down by the relevant planning authority. It always helps if your objections are backed up by others – numbers do count.

Mr Harold Woolfson,   March 5
MP for Upper Craddock,
House of Commons,
Parliament Square,
London SW1

Dear Mr Woolfson,

As one of your constituents (and supporters) I hope you can help in the following matter.

Last December it was learned that funding for the Special Needs Department of Lambert Comprehensive School was to be frozen at the 1997 level despite a 40% increase in students requiring special educational needs help. Although normally funding is the responsibility of the East Sussex Education Department it seems to have no control over the situation.

As the chairwoman of an ad hoc committee of concerned parents I have been unsuccessful, despite three months of trying, in identifying which government department is responsible for effectively cutting the funding for a vital educational service.

Copies of all correspondence is attached and I would appreciate it if you could help us understand what is going on and whom to approach to correct this absurd situation.

Yours faithfully,

Emma Clarkson

Writing to a Member of Parliament

- Your MP is a kind of court of last resort so it is expected that you will have exhausted every avenue before approaching him or her.

- Keep your submission short and to the point and attach copies of relevant documents. It saves time if you are sure of your facts. Try to make clear what it is you want your MP to do.

- An MP may not be able or in the position to change the course of history but most will do what they can to help; their jobs, after all, depend upon people like you.

Staying alive: Employer and Employee

Work is accomplished by those employees who have not yet reached their level of incompetence.

The Peter Principle

In the workplace, employer and employee face a two-way trial. When a job advertisement appears these days, the odds are that it will attract dozens, sometimes hundreds, of applications. The employer (or the personnel manager) then faces the task of sifting through the mass of paper trying to pick a winner. The would-be employee, on the other hand, is an entrant in a race that is not necessarily won by the swift but more often by ingenuity and guile.

For the employer, knowing what he or she wants makes the task easier. The wise employer will advertise a precise job description and all applications will be compared to that. People who seem closest to the ideal will be ahead in the race.

If you're an applicant whose qualifications, experience and personal profile fit the job description you're in there with a chance. You might be among the final half-dozen, but there is only one vacancy. So what are the factors – the 'special extras' – that will provide that surge to get you to the finishing line first?

At the interview stage there is a good chance that, of several equally qualified finalists, the applicant with a pleasant appearance, exuding self-confidence and a winning charm is most likely to get the job. But less-presentable applicants can do quite a lot about more subtle presentational skills – such as writing enviably clear, persuasive, attention-getting letters. In short, expressing and enhancing their personalities through the written word. Qualities such as enthusiasm, clarity of thought, confidence and know-how can all be conveyed to a reader by a well-written letter.

Enlightened employers know how fewer and fewer recruits can communicate well. Perhaps illiteracy has been largely overcome, but semi-literacy is all around us. So be assured that good speakers and skilled writers will always be in demand.

If you are a job-seeker, this section will try to help you develop some basic writing skills that should help you get a job, and keep it. The section also includes tips on preparing and presenting a **CV** (your resume of education, professional or vocational training and work experience, or **curriculum vitae**).

Getting that Job – Some Preliminaries

Before starting on your written application, find out as much as you can about the firm or organisation, and its business. Ask for any brochures they may have. A knowledgeable applicant will win hands down over one who has no idea what the employer actually does.

Don't waste your time, or the employer's, by responding to an advertisement for a job if it requires qualifications you don't really have. Send your CV with a covering letter explaining why you think you are suitable for the job, and state where you saw the job advertised. It is customary to offer, references though not to enclose them with your initial application. Ask to be considered for an interview.

Don't make claims that won't stand up. By all means emphasise your strong points, especially those relevant to the job, but don't lie. Don't claim extensive experience if your lack of it will soon become embarrassingly apparent. If you do lack experience, emphasise your enthusiasm, adaptability and willingness to learn.

Before despatching your application check it thoroughly – several times – for neatness and correctness. Make sure there are no spelling errors, especially in the firm's or organisation's name; these can make many employers grind their teeth and toss your application on the reject pile. Keep copies of your covering letter and CV.

Your application may be, not a response to an advertised job, but a letter enquiring if there is a vacancy. In this case make sure your covering letter is addressed to the right person, by name or title or both. If in doubt, call the firm's switchboard. Emphasise your willingness to be interviewed and that you are prepared to wait until an appropriate job does become vacant. Enclose your CV and ask if it can be filed to await a vacancy.

Be specific about your training, qualifications and work experience. A 'course in cookery' could mean anything to a hotel wanting a trainee chef; a 'Master Chef's Federation Catering Certificate' could attract serious attention. Don't claim to have 'worked for several electrical contractors'; name them and also say when they employed you.

Personnel Manager   February 16
Bush Paper Products Ltd,
Saxon Industrial Estate,
Aberdeen AB3 7UU

Dear Sir,

     I am responding to your advertisement in the Feb 13 edition of the 'Sunday Post' for a Technical Support Manager.

     The position is just what I have been looking for and from the job description I am sure I have the requisite training and experience. My CV is attached.

     Although I am happy and reasonably well-paid in my present job there are few opportunities for advancement. I have studied at night for an Grade 2 Supervisor's Diploma and now feel I am ready for a fresh challenge.

I am aware that your company is highly innovative and growing and I am sure I can play a part in its future success.

     I live locally, am happily married with two children, and genuinely see my future in the paper products industry.

     I look forward to hearing from you and can make myself available for interview any day except Fridays.

Yours faithfully,

Richard McCormick

Applying for an Advertised Job

- This would be regarded as an intelligent covering letter for a CV. Without frills, it projects ambition, enthusiasm, conscientiousness and stability – presumably the qualities in a job applicant every employer is looking for.

- If you think it helps, a brief paragraph about your family status (stability) and interest in the employer's industry (devotion) can be included, as above.

- Always explain why you wish to leave your present job.

The Personnel Manager,   July 22
Balcombe Industries Ltd,
Maybank Road,
Torquay TQ2 9JR,

Dear Sir,

     I am writing to enquire whether there are any openings in your company for a Packaging Materials Technical Officer, either now or in the near future.

     At present I am employed as a Technical Trainee at a packaging materials firm but feel that my training and experience now qualify me for advancement opportunities not available from my present employer.

     My CV is attached and you will see that I have spent the past six years on materials courses and training seminars.

     I now feel I am ready for a position of greater responsibility with opportunities for growth which I hope might be available at Balcombe Industries.

     I look forward to a favourable reply and can make myself available for interview at almost any time.

Yours faithfully,

Simon Masters

Enquiring about Job Opportunities

- The big hurdle facing a letter like this is simply that there may be no immediate job prospects at all. But there may be in the future – and there is always the chance that your letter might be filed and referred to if that happy situation should come about.

- Keep your letter short, snappy and above all, optimistic. Try to convey an impression of a person who is well-qualified, hard-working and eager to face the challenge of a new and more rewarding job.

Mr Brian Haydon,
Managing Director, January 14
Haydon & Bright Opticians,
High St, Norwich NR1 6TD.

Dear Mr Haydon,

I understand there may be a vacancy in your firm for an experienced optical assistant.

I have spent 12 years working as an optometrist's assistant, both in the front of the shop and in optical labs. I also have extensive experience in dealing with the public and their optical problems and hold an optometrist's testing certificate. The attached CV gives a detailed account of my qualifications and experience.

Although I have not worked full-time for nearly nine years (raising my family of three girls) I have tons of energy and enthusiasm. I also think I can prove I am conscientious and reliable and I get on famously with people whether they are colleagues or customers. I look forward to hearing from you soon.

Yours sincerely,

Janet Macpherson

Rejoining the Work Force

- For complex and obscure reasons many employers are biassed against people who are over 40, declared redundant or otherwise out of work. Perhaps they're thought to be losers. On the contrary, most are industrious and enterprising, and undeserving of their plight.

- So your letter must defuse this latent hostility by painting a picture of an employee bubbling with the energy and enthusiasm of youth but with the wisdom and experience of maturity.

12 Upper Town Street,
Luton, LU23 7GN
August 31

Mrs Belinda Penney
Personnel Department,
Cross Department Stores Ltd,
Draper Rd, Luton LU4 4RD

Dear Mrs Penney,

Thank you for your letter inviting me for an interview for the position of Systems Analyst at your Luton head office.

I am pleased to confirm that I am available for the interview at 10am, Tuesday, September 8.

I look forward to meeting you then.

Yours sincerely,

Sarah Addison

Confirming an Interview

- If you get as far as being offered an interview, don't assume it's all over. It's not. You may be the only candidate, or you may have a dozen or more rivals. That's why it's worthwhile making a good impression when accepting or confirming your interview.

- Make it crisp and businesslike and perhaps just a touch – but just a touch – grateful.

Mr George Bashford,   April 18
General Manager,
Cranbrook Hilton Hotel.

Dear Mr Bashford,

I would like to ask for a review of my salary which, as you know, has remained unchanged during the three years I have worked as Booking Manager of the hotel.

In that time I believe I have worked hard and competently. My range of duties has also grown; on Mondays and Tuesdays I have the extra responsibilities of the switchboard and opening the cocktail bar in the afternoons. I often fill in for absent staff on weekends. I believe you have never heard a complaint against me and after three years here I am now an experienced and more efficient employee.

However none of the above has been rewarded even though our room occupancy rate has increased by 18% in that time.

I hope you will recognise my worth to the hotel with an appropriate increase in my salary.

Yours sincerely,

Harry Adams, Front Desk

Asking for a Salary Increase

- It shouldn't happen of course, but it does: many employers never grant salary increases unless they're really pressed. If you find yourself in the position of a salary supplicant here are some points that may help your case:

- Stress the length of time your salary has remained static.

- List any extra responsibilities you've taken on in that time.

- Point out that in that time you've gained the experience which has made you more efficient and productive at your job.

- If your employer is doing well in terms of sales or profit, point out that you, as an employee, helped contribute to that, and should be rewarded.

Mr David Black,   June 30
Chief Executive,
Forward & Thomas Engineering plc,
Oldham.

Dear David,

     I regret to tell you that I have decided to resign from my present position of Senior Designer in the Fabrication Unit. I wish to leave at the end of July and therefore give you the four weeks' notice as required by the terms of my contract.

     Although I am accepting a position with one of our competitors I have genuinely enjoyed my six years working with you and hope I've given the company as much as it's given me in experience and creative satisfaction. However the new position gives me a wider range of responsibilities with appropriate financial rewards and I simply could not pass up the opportunity.

     Thank you for your past support and a friendship that I hope will endure beyond this parting of the ways.

Yours sincerely,

Simon Felstead

Tendering Your Resignation

- Unless the circumstances leading to your decision to quit are acrimonious, don't burn any bridges. Often a polite and sincerely felt letter of resignation will make management think again, perhaps leading to your reappointment on much more favourable terms.

- If you've enjoyed working for the company, say so. You might also refer to your reasons for leaving. And if your departure leaves the company in the lurch, an offer to train a replacement will go down well.

- Retaining goodwill keeps the door open for the possibility of returning to the firm in the future, and also helps when you ask for a reference.

March 20

14 Flanagan Drive
Hopetown Park,
Hull, HU5 2TG

Rev Walter McDonnell,
The Rectory,
Hopetown Parade,
Hull.

Dear Rev. McDonnell,

I am applying for the position of deputy retail manager at Carson's Electrical Stores in Hull, and wonder if you would be kind enough to supply me with a reference.

Although I am not a regular churchgoer, I am one of your parishioners and we have met on several occasions at social events.

I enclose my CV for your reference so you will see that I am a hard-working father and that I have worked on several community projects. The new job means a lot to me, especially the higher pay, as I have been very hard-pressed financially during the past few years.

Yours sincerely,

Trevor Evans

Asking for a Reference

- Employers and recruitment professionals are generally agreed on the importance of references, which can act as a kind of 'proof of existence' for the candidate's virtues. A job application accompanied by several references will usually be taken seriously.

- If asking for a reference give the referee some guidance on what should be stressed. In the above example the writer has enclosed his CV which gives the referee some meat to work on.

Stein Electronics Pty Ltd
Border Leas, Chelmsford, Essex CM2 7AY
Executive Offices

May 12

TO WHOM IT MAY CONCERN

I have known Miss Joanna Patrick for six years, since she came to work for Stein Electronics, Chelmsford, in April 1992, as personal assistant to the sales director.

During this time she has been an enthusiastic, supportive and hard-working executive – the complete professional. Her personal contribution to this company has been considerable, and she will be missed both as a valued colleague and friend.

Any organisation fortunate enough to recruit Joanna will find her a highly intelligent, fast-thinking, loyal and devoted employee. Joanna is energetic and ambitious and intends to widen her experience in electronics sales, and she leaves with our best wishes.

Sincerely,

Jeremy Woodstock, Executive Chairman

Writing a Reference or Testimonial

- Most references are coded; enthusiasms tend to be muted, flaws are glossed over and weaknesses of character are expressed in the best light. So if you really want to praise someone you have to break the mould to try to ensure that your reference is read as sincere and truthful.

- Rather than write a potentially damaging though truthful reference – which could result in a libel action – make an excuse and leave the testimonial writing to others.

Selling Yourself: Creating a persuasive CV

Avoid what we call a 'Carmen Miranda' CV – like the words of her famous song it has too much 'I, I, I, I'. . .

Recruitment Consultant

Most people would find it extremely difficult to tell their life story to a complete stranger. To tell it on paper could prove to be even more difficult. So it isn't surprising that many job seekers respond to ads in the recruitment columns of newspapers and turn to professional writing services to create their CVs. Even then, results can be uncertain and sometimes a waste of time and money.

Yet you can write an effective curriculum vitae by following some simple rules.

First, **presentation**. A CV should be well laid out, attractive to the eye; typed or prepared on a word processor using either a 12pt or 14pt typeface; and preferably not more than two pages long. Good quality paper can help to give a good initial impression. You'll probably need a dozen or so clean, clear copies.

Second, **stick to the facts**. Divide the CV into essential sections: **personal details**, **education and training**, **employment and career**, **professional profile**, **useful talents** and **attributes**. The order of these sections is a matter of taste. Some prefer personal details (name, age, address, marital status, etc) at the beginning of a CV; others at the end. However, your employment record – the jobs you've held, right up to your present one – is of most interest to an employer and should command pride of position. Including the names and contact addresses or telephone numbers of referees is optional but you should certainly say that references can be supplied on request if you have them.

Personal details:

Full name, address, phone number.

Employment and Career:

Lead off with details of your present or most recent job. If you have had several jobs over a period of years, give more details about the most recent, less information about your earlier employment. Supply start and end dates of each of your jobs. Keep the summaries brief: name of employer, location, type of work involved, and possibly the reason you moved on.

Education and Training:

Include brief details of secondary education, names of schools, colleges, dates of attendence, exam passes from GCSE/Standard Grade upwards, any special merits. Add to this details of any university courses or degrees, and any other qualifications – for example business school courses, technical or vocational training, etc.

Personal and Professional Profile:

While your employment record and educational qualifications provide an objective summary of your current status as a job-seeker, a prospective employer also needs to have an analysis of your personality and skills. If you believe yourself to be pleasant, optimistic, competitive and cooperative with good communication abilities, then say so. Are you recognised as a good team worker? A leader? Are you creative and outgoing, or do you possess a quieter, more analytical nature? If you think certain qualities are relevant to the job you're applying for, stick them in. Then outline the skills you've learned during your work experience – flesh out your job descriptions with instances of specific attainments, workplace innovations, sales records, management commendations and so on.

Other Attributes:

Here you could list such lifestyle bonuses as having a clean driving licence, fluency in a foreign language, computer proficiency, etc.

Personal Details:

List your age and birth date, nationality, marital status and number of children, state of health and, if you really must, personal interests, preferably intellectual (chess); cultural (choir singing); sport (rugby referee, golf); relaxation (gardening). Don't say you're a theatregoer even if you are; everybody does.

Try to cover all this in two pages if you can. If you can't, revise; deciding what to leave out can be as important as what you put in. Check and double-check for spelling errors and grammatical gaffes. Don't make moral judgments about yourself; passages such as 'I am kind and considerate with an unblemished record of honesty' are out. Don't lie: you'll eventually be rumbled. Don't belittle previous employers or reveal confidential information such as sales figures and production plans. Faxing your job application and CV as well as mailing them can help you get noticed.

Remember that you are marketing **you**. You're both salesperson and product. You have an intimate knowledge of the product and how good it is. Now get out there and sell yourself!

Marianne Jane Craig
42 Nettlehome Drive, Curnow Park,
Bournemough BH8 5TG
01202 566 876

CURRICULUM VITAE

Employment:
* March 1996 to present:
  Sales Director, Floor Coverings Division, Viscose Corporation, London.
  Responsible for national sales team of 16 reps and overseas agents in 22 countries.
* January 1992-March 1996: Sales Manager, Heritage Furnishings, Leeds.
  Responsible for national sales of all company products; led sales team of 7.
* April 1991-January 1992: Senior Sales Representative, Heritage Furnishings.
* May 1990-April 1991: Sales Representative, Heritage Furnishings.
* September 1988-May 1990: Sales Trainee Optimum Fabrics Ltd, Manchester.

Education:
St Stephen's College, Manchester 1979-86; 8 O-levels; 2 A-levels (History B; English B)
Manchester Union Art College 1986-88; Design Diploma; Fabric Design Certificate.

Career Profile:
My interest in design and fabrics led me into the furnishings trade where because
of my technical and art training I was offered a trainee sales position. From that
point my career has grown to the point where I am now responsible for national
and international sales of a range of innovative floor coverings (sales in 1997
£31.6m); building the brands; marketing strategy and advertising agency liaison
(3 accounts billing £2.8m) – all figures on trade record. I now believe my experience
and success have prepared me for a broader-based executive sales position,
preferably with an international home products company.

Personal Profile:
I have always been regarded as a good team worker which I believe has helped me
to lead and inspire sales teams. I enjoy my work and it never worries me that I put
in many extra hours a week of my own time. I am computer literate and write and
design most of the company's sales literature. I am quite competitive and have won
several sales awards during my career.

Other:
I have a clean driver's licence. I have no problem relocating either in the UK or
overseas. I am at present half-way through a part-time MBA course with the
Open University.

Personal:
Age 31. Born 16/10/1967
British nationality
Formerly married six years; now divorced; one 5-year old child (girl)
Health excellent
Interests: tennis, patio gardening

Documentation:
Full sales history and detailed responsibilities can be supplied on request.
References available on request.

That's a fairly straightforward CV, with lots to shout about and nothing to hide. It portrays a bright and talented young lady who'd be an asset to any sales-oriented company, and she shouldn't have to wait too long before she's snapped up.

But not everyone is so fortunate. Let's take a young man whose CV, if it's to be an honest document, has to reflect some knocks: a period of illness, say, another of unemployment, and an incomplete education. The challenge here is, in the words of the popular song, to 'accentuate the positive' while not completely 'eliminating the negative'. See how it looks.

Charles Timothy Renwick
23A Vaucluse Road,
Portergate, Slough SL5 7JK

CURRICULUM VITAE

October 1995 - March 1998. ASSISTANT PRODUCTION MANAGER
Rickard & Packer Industrial Lithographers, Slough. Supervised work-flow through 4 AB Mann 6-colour units, plus folders, binding, finishing, packing, store and despatch. Was due to be made Production Mgr (have reference to this effect) but because of lack of orders two units closed down and I was made redundant.

September 1992 - October 1997. DEPUTY PRODUCTION MANAGER
Clayburn & Son, Book Printers, Reading. Responsible for all book throughput and quality control, binding, finishing and despatch. Volume ranged from 2m to 2.7 million units per month. Was offered temporary Assistant Production Manager position at Rickard & Packer, and promised Production Manager position there at end of 1998.

February 1991 - September 1992. DEPUTY MANAGER, BINDERY
Clayburn & Son, Book Printers, Reading. Took over from former Deputy Manager who was promoted. This gave me almost two years valuable experience in case-binding and paperbacking techniques. Responsible for maintenance and staff of 23.

April 1990 - February 1991. GENERAL ASSISTANT, BINDERY
Clayburn & Son, Book Printers, Reading. Relocated to Reading. Although could not get a job in line with my printing trade skills I was keen to add bookbinding to my work experience.

December 1989 - March 1990. CLEANER
Southern Printers Pty Ltd, Southampton. Best job I could get after my illness but it did keep me in touch with the printing trade.

From March to December 1989 I suffered from a severe back injury sustained during my employment with Industrial Packaging. During this time I was unable to work but managed to complete a home study course on Computer Data Processing.

September 1985 - December 1989. STORE CLERK
Industrial Packaging Printers Ltd, Southampton. Moved to Southampton to improve employment prospects but the store job was the best offering. Printing trade generally very depressed. During July 1984 to September 1985 I was unemployed, apart from some part-time work on local farms. I completed a 1-year night course on Computing at Maidstone Technical College.

September 1980 - July 1984. LEADING HAND LITHO PRINTER
Otway Greeting Cards Ltd, Maidstone, Kent. Responsible for pre-prep and running of Butler colour web press. Won commendation and bonus for increasing volume 20% two years running. Firm was taken over by Hanways in 1984 and all operations moved to Bristol. Was made redundant.

January 1980 - September 1980. LITHO PRESS TRAINEE
Otway Greeting Cards Ltd, Maidstone, Kent.

EDUCATION
Paddock Wood Comprehensive 1972-78, 2 O-levels. 1978-1980 Youth Training Centre, Maidstone, General Printing Course Certificate. Vocational Training, Maidstone Technical College, Lithographic Press Operator Proficiency Diploma.

PERSONAL AND CAREER PROFILE
I am an optimistic person, enjoy working hard, and am motivated to improve myself. I am particularly interested in printing and new printing technology including digital processes. I have moved three times in order to stay in the trade which is where I believe my future lies. I now have the knowledge, experience and maturity to enable me to take on management responsibilities in all phases of print production.

PERSONAL DETAILS
Age: 36. Born January 13, 1962.
Married 1984; four children, aged 13, 11, 8, 5.
Health: Good. Wear supportive brace for back injury.
Nationality: British
Clean driving licence; Commercial Vehicle license.
Personal Interests: Coach Slough Central High football team; fly fishing.

Mr Renwick's CV plainly states the bald truth that during his working life he's had six months off work through injury and a spell of unemployment lasting over a year. And, having recently been made redundant, he's out of work right now.

But despite what might be considered by some employers as drawbacks, the CV manages to depict Mr Renwick as a conscientious worker determined to make good in his chosen field, the printing industry. It demonstrates how he used his time off work usefully by undertaking computer courses, and how he overcame employment setbacks by moving to where work for a printer was available. And, if you follow the ups and downs of his career there is a steady upward line of progress from trainee to middle management. A thoughtful employer, reading the CV carefully, could hardly fail to be impressed by the qualities of this perhaps unspectacular, but industrious artisan.

Could a real-life Charles Renwick write such a document? Why not? If you analyse the CV it is really nothing more than a collection of facts – employers, job descriptions, dates, educational and personal details, arranged in logical order and presented so that it is easy to read and absorb.

Anyone can do it – and, if ever the need presents itself – so can you.

Getting it and keeping it: Money matters

That money talks, I'll not deny, I heard it once: it said 'Goodbye'.

Richard Armour

Previous chapters have touched on money matters (chasing a loan, p.163; querying a bank statement, p.179; terminating a hire-purchase agreement, p.184; pleading inability to pay, p.187, etc) but here we'll take a closer look at how the stuff that dominates our lives can be made, lost and kept with the help of the written word.

Losing it is distressingly easy. Losing it when it isn't your fault is just plain distressing. Unless you're a hermit it's almost impossible these days to live without a favourable credit rating, and gathering and supplying information about a citizen's creditworthiness is a huge business. Naturally, they can get it wrong, and every day several thousand people suddenly have the feeling that they're walking around with a big sign over their heads saying: 'Won't Pay, Don't Lend', even though they've never renaged on a debt in their lives. The salesperson who's about to wrap up your purchase makes a phone call and shakes her head. The bank manager's frostiness matches the glass panels of his office. The word is out: you're a financial pariah.

If this Kafkaesque situation ever happens to you, start writing. First, to whoever refused your application for credit – whether a store, credit card organisation, bank or hire-purchase company – requesting to be told the specific reason for being turned down.

No organisation offering credit need give any reasons for refusing credit, but you do have some protection under the Consumer Credit Act 1974 (Sections 157-160) if they have based the refusal on information supplied by a credit reference agency, which it commonly is. Your letter might look like this:

December 14

The Manager,
Credit Control Office,
Sanders, Sachs Finance Co Ltd,
London, E1 5BD

Dear Sir/Madam,

Yesterday my application to buy a 28 inch colour TV from Mason's Electronics through a two-year hire-purchase agreement with your firm was refused.

I would like to know the reason for the refusal because I have no unpaid debts and my current bank account is in credit.

If the refusal is related in any way to information supplied by a credit reference agency you are bound by the Consumer Credit Act 1974 to advise me of the name of that agency in order that the information may be checked.

I would appreciate your prompt cooperation in this and look forward to hearing from you.

Yours faithfully,

Arnold L Travers

Credit Refusal

- A letter like that, providing it is delivered within 28 days of the refusal, is the first step in banishing the bête noir of uncreditworthiness.

- The urgency is quite real, because even the fact that you were refused a hire-purchase loan (perhaps based on misinformation) can finish up as a blot on your credit record.

- The second step is to write to the agency concerned to request a copy of the file they keep of your your credit record:

The Manager,   December 20
Credit Report Services Ltd,
Bishopsgate, London E2 4RF

Dear Sir/Madam,

On December 13 I was refused credit through a hire-purchase
agreement by Sanders, Sachs Finance Co Ltd. They have informed me,
as required by the Consumer Credit Act 1974, that their refusal was based
on credit information about me that was supplied by you.

As there is nothing in my financial history that could warrant
such a refusal I believe your records are wrong and under the above Act I
request a copy of my complete credit file, held by you, without delay.
If any charges are involved please let me know.

Yours faithfully,

Arnold L Travers

Requesting Your Credit History

- Under the Consumer Credit Act 1974, credit reference and
  investigation agencies are required to give you all the information
  about you that they have on file. If this information is incorrect you
  can take steps to have it withdrawn or revised. With your credit
  rating restored there will be thousands of lenders out there only too
  willing to give you money.

Next to losing your reputation as an A-class credit risk, losing or
having your credit cards stolen – along with the probability that someone is
having a shopping spree at your expense – can induce justified panic.
Depending upon the fine print on your credit card agreement you are liable for
all or most of the pecuniary damage if you don't notify the issuers of its loss.
The important point here is, of course, to phone the issuing organisation
immediately, but then to follow up with a confirmatory letter with all the
details:

The Manager, July 15
Card Services,
Standard Northern Bank plc,
PO Box 23,
Brighton BN2 6TG

Dear Sir/Madam,

Standard Northern Bank Payment Card 6802 8492 2241 5144

This will confirm my advice by phone this morning that the above card, in my name, is missing.

I last used it for purchasing petrol at the Phoenix Garage, Whitstable, Kent, at about 6.30pm on July 14 and first noticed it missing at 9.30am on July 15.

I would appreciate it if you would arrange to send me a replacement card as soon as possible.

Yours faithfully,

George N Wheedon

So much for trying to keep your money. Spending it is easy. Buying is child's play. But selling . . .

One of the laws of life is that, sooner or later, you have to sell something, to become a salesperson. Perhaps it's flogging your ageing car, or the abandoned greenhouse, in the local freesheet. Or finding customers for a child-minding service . . . tempting people out on a cold winter's night to attend a fund-raising event, or to bring and buy at a church fête . . . finding buyers for your self-published history of the village, or for your dried herbs and flowers . . . whether it's persuading someone to do something or buy something, it all requires salesmanship. Some of us are good at it ('he's a natural salesman . . could sell refrigerators to Eskimos') but most of us are not. Which prompts the question: can salesmanship be taught?

The existence of thousands of sales training books, programmes, classes, seminars, colleges and even degree courses suggests that it can be. Certainly the principles of successful selling can be learned and put to use, either in direct selling (one-to-one personal contact), 'cold calling' or telesales, or by the written word.

The Sales Letter

Whether you are a one-off, part-time, semi-professional or professional salesperson the aim is the same – to sell. But before we embark on the theory and practice of selling, there are some preliminaries. Are there people out there who might want what you have to sell? And if so, who are they? Where are they?

Unless you get satisfactory answers to these questions, you could be wasting your time, no matter how wonderful your product or service, or how brilliant your prose.

Most businesses try to establish the saleability of a product or service by test-marketing. This especially applies to selling by mail and is usually done by sampling, or sending out mailshots to selected targets – to different residential areas, for example; or to people grouped by occupation; or to commercially available lists of people who have previously purchased a similar product or service. The results of these sample mailshots are monitored; eventually a picture emerges of the kind of person most likely to become a buyer. This testing process helps to define the market for the particular product or service and eliminates the waste of sending expensive mail to households who wouldn't be interested.

With the help of test-marketing you, as the writer, should have a clear idea of whoever you hope to win as a customer. As with any letter, a sales letter – although it might finish up in a million homes – must make the readers feel that it is personally addressed to him or her. To touch a nerve, hit an emotional soft spot, appeal to the senses or the mind, to give your arguments any conviction, you must write as an individual to an individual. And what you write must be relevant to the recipient's interests. If your targets are, say, busy mothers with children, to whom you intend selling a vacuum cleaner, it will be pointless to confuse them with the diameter of the wheels or the horsepower of the motor. You would stress qualities such as efficiency, lightness in weight, clever accessories, attractiveness and lack of maintenance problems.

Whether your sales pitch is in the form of a letter, circular, brochure, poster or advertisement, the structure usually consists of three elements:

THE HEADLINE – to attract attention and interest
THE ARGUMENT – the description, need, usefulness, value
THE ENDING – the personal appeal, the deal, the clincher

Each of these elements is capable of endless variation. The approach can be gently persuasive or about as subtle as a steamroller; pleading or deliberately off-hand; understated or extravagant. But whatever the approach, the piece should be attractive and inviting to the eye. This helps, but is far from fool-proof. Every writer of sales literature has to get used to the brutal fact that 98% of the population abhors unsolicited sales bumpf and bins it without a second glance. The average response (not necessarily sales) to unsolicited mail or leaflets is less than 2% – that is, two people out of every 100 might be sufficiently interested in your proposition to respond at all. So how can you beat the odds?

Your chances of beating those odds are governed by your choice of approach. There are no rules, which is why mail order and leafleting is largely a matter of trial and error; if one approach doesn't succeed, you try another. If it does score some success, you continue to refine your approach, to see if you can improve results even further. It's trial, trial and trial again.

So let's see how all this vague theory can actually be applied to real situations. Let's take three products:

- A home-gym muscle-toning machine costing £249
- A grow-your-own herbs window box costing £19.99
- A local news-oriented radio station, CHAT-FM

The Opening – and the Selling Concept

With each product we'll try various approaches, first with the opening, or headline:

The Challenge
Home Gym: *How would you like to feel fitter, look better, in just 14 days?*
Herb Box: *Like to grow herbs – without ever getting your hands dirty?*
CHAT-FM: *Become a smarter, more interesting person!*

The Amazing Fact
Home Gym: *You have 436 muscles. Half of them are probably out of shape.*
Herb Box: *Now you can grow the 'Secret of Life' herb.*
CHAT-FM: *CHAT-FM carries more news than 7 national newspapers.*

The Invitation
Home Gym: *Try this Home Gym for two weeks – at our expense.*
Herb Box: *You can own a unique scented garden for just £19.99.*
CHAT-FM: *Talk direct to your MP on CHAT-FM this week.*

The Case History
Home Gym: *Frank : 'I lost 5 pounds in just a week with Home Gym'*
Herb Box: *'I can open my window on to a perfumed garden.'*
CHAT-FM: *'CHAT-FM is my constant companion.'*

Remember when . . .
Home Gym: *When did you last run up three flights of stairs?*
Herb Box: *Herbs to bring the old-style taste back into your cooking.*
CHAT-FM: *Remember when people actually listened to radio?*

You're Number One
Home Gym: *You know you want to be fitter, leaner, sharper, better.*
Herb Box: *You've always wanted a herb garden. Here it is, £19.99.*
CHAT-FM: *Phone us any time. We want to hear your opinion.*

The Bribe
Home Gym: *Two free home fitness videos with every Home Gym.*
Herb Box: *Free copy of 'Herb Gardening' with every order.*
CHAT-FM: *Listen to CHAT-FM 'News Clues' - win a Summer Holiday.*

Many copywriters begin with a 'concept' approach to their task, jotting down a selection of selling lines each representing a different appeal, a different approach. Which one is likely to fit the product or service best? Which is likely to appeal to the target market? Who, for example, are we likely to be talking to about the Home Gym?

Probably health-conscious, 24-44 year olds, both male and female, people prepared to spend £249 and an hour or two a day toning up their bodies. So forget the nostalgic approach. Would this group respond to a challenge? Possibly. Would they believe a testimonial? Possibly. Or are we looking at people who think about themselves a lot, who are conscious of their well-being and appearance? Probably – in which case the 'You're Number One' approach would seem to be a good fit: You know you want to be fitter, leaner, sharper, better!

Who's likely to buy the window box herb garden? Here we can picture a woman, probably a housewife, who spends a lot of time captive in the kitchen and who might like to nurture a mini-garden of herbs outside her kitchen window. She would also be likely to have £19.99 in disposable income to buy it, too. So why don't we pitch to her? The 'invitation' approach seems appropriate, or we might idealise our prospect in a fictional case history (for they are rarely true!) as a glamorous young woman reaching out to her prolific kitchen window garden and picking a bunch of scented herbs to flavour an exotic meal she's cooking: *Mmm! I just open my kitchen window to a Mediterranean garden.*

A radio station has to sell its service to as many listeners as it can reach. CHAT-FM is a news and talk station, but not over-serious or ponderous. It's looking for listeners who want to be up-to-date with the news and to be informed, but who also enjoy light, chatty content and even involvement in the station's phone-in sessions. How can we best reach these potential listeners, and to win them over from other radio stations?

If CHAT-FM possesses a USP (unique selling point) then we should use it; in this case it is the claim that the station carries more news in a day 'than seven national daily newspapers'. Sounds good, but will it be enough? Perhaps we should add a bribe to persuade people to switch: CHAT-FM gives you more news than seven national newspapers – plus a summer holiday in Bermuda!

With the selling approach settled, we must now see if it fits the product or service – and the argument or proposition. Don't get the idea that creating winning sales copy is a matter of writing-by-numbers. It isn't. Although you are dealing with lots of separate elements, the finished product must be a seamless, unified creation.

The Steak – and the Sizzle

Now we come to the product or service itself – what it is, what makes it better than similar products, what benefits will be derived from it, why it is good value for money, why buying it represents little or no risk. Here, there is no substitute for a thorough knowledge, understanding and appreciation of the product or service; it's very difficult to write credible, convincing sales copy if you don't know what you're talking about.

After not only studying the Home Gym but also using it, you may note that it has some interesting, if not unique, advantages. Exercising with it is almost a pleasure: it can adapt to over 40 exercises for the body's muscles. It is light to transport, but sturdily built, and stows away easily. It has a built-in timer and electronic weight scales. It can adjust to people of different heights and weights. Compared to other, similar apparatus it is excellent value for money. And it can be bought with easy payments over 12 months.

Some of these attributes might be more important to our target market than others, which may affect the way you give prominence to them in your copy, but they are all worth developing. The manufacturer claims that although most features can be found on other home-gym machines, the electronic weighing platform is unique, allowing the user to tell, within a gram, how much weight is lost after each session. It sounds like the kind of extra that could tweak a potential customer's arm enough to want to buy it.

The maker is also willing to allow a free two-week trial; if the buyer isn't satisfied, the machine can be returned for a full refund. That's worth highlighting, too, because it demonstrates the manufacturer's faith in the product. Present it as a copper-bottomed, no-risk guarantee. It all adds up to a valid, serviceable, value-for-money item with plenty of interesting selling points.

The Herb Garden Window Box is a deep, green-painted aluminium tray with 20 small packets of different herb seeds, a bag of special compost and a booklet of growing instructions – not really much to look at. What you are selling here is not the steak, but the sizzle – the dream of a summer windowsill lush with fragrant herbs that can be plucked fresh for the table. So, develop the benefits: the visual delight of the mini-garden, the different characters and uses of the herbs, the perfume redolent of hot Mediterranean lands, not to mention how the oregano will perk up meat dishes and how a few sprigs of spearmint will add dash to a salad. All this for just £19.99 – plus a free book on herbs and herb gardening if you buy early.

Radio stations try to 'position' themselves to appeal to a particular market – to forge a union of product and image designed to appeal to the kind of listener they wish to attract and retain. CHAT-FM Radio is a new local station, competing against the national BBC stations, Classic-FM and several regionals. It has set out to provide strong local services: hourly news, market, traffic and weather reports, plus national and international news updates.

Music is minimal and listeners can phone in to daily discussions. The format is unhurried but ordered and efficient. But is that enough to entice listeners to switch from other stations. Probably not.

Now the writer has to become a detective, to search for that elusive USP. If it can't be found or doesn't exist, it can be created. With CHAT-FM, success may come in the form of a team of bright, young announcers, devoted and enthusiastic. So why don't you sell 'The Chat Team'? Like the Spice Girls or the Teletubbies, each member of the team has a distinct personality that can be developed. Encourage listeners, potential and listeners, to get to know them and love them. Identify and then develop certain aspects of their personalities and lifestyles. Who's the Lothario? The agony aunt? The presenter with the Robin Reliant? The weather girl who hates getting her hair wet? Now you're giving flesh and faces to the radio station. Now you have something concrete to sell.

The Close – and the Clincher

You have their attention, you've whetted their interest, you've described the product or service, you've presented the benefits, you've convinced them of the extraordinary value and alerted them to a unique opportunity. Then you lose them. What's gone wrong?

Preventing that from happening is the job of the finale, the close, the clincher. A hundred thousand people might see an ad for a theatrical play. Ten thousand might express interest. A thousand of these might read a favourable review of the play and decide they'd like to see it. Of these, eight hundred, for one reason or another, can't go. Things are pretty desperate! How do you persuade the remaining two hundred?

Advertising copywriters generally agree that it's not difficult to plant an idea in a person's mind. The idea might be, 'Yes, I really like that watch. I'd love to have one. Not all that expensive, either? Mmm . . .' The difficulty is to provoke action.

Try to look into the mind of the health-conscious, 35-year-old shoe-store manager who's read your mailshot on the Home Gym. She's thought about acquiring such a machine for some time. She has the space, and the money to buy it. She likes the look of the Home Gym and appreciates all its features. So why . . . why doesn't she complete the coupon or phone up with her credit card number? If you, the writer, were the salesman, face-to-face with this woman, you'd instinctively know that you were within a hair's breadth of making the sale. What would you do to close the deal? That's how you have to think if you're writing sales copy. So, what would you do?

Well, you could try offering a 10% discount, which would translate in a sales letter as something like: If we receive your order within 7 days we'll give you 10% discount – you'll save £24.90! Or you could throw in a gift, or bonus: Get a free pair of Easigrip hand weights worth £21! Marketers and advertisers know that the well-chosen clincher can increase response by 200% and more.

With an item such as the herb-garden window box you are, as we noted, selling a dream rather than a tray of soil and some seeds. So offering a discount isn't what it's really about here – you need to expand and embroider the dream. A small, romantic, illustrated book about the mystery of herbs could work. Or perhaps a free pomander or sachet of pillow herbs to promote sleep. Let's see how this might look: For the first 1,000 orders – FREE! – this Victorian pomander of fragrant pillow herbs to transport you to a deep, dreamy slumber.

A broadcasting service is already free to its listeners, so you can't exploit the freebie option. So what device will be capable of motivating a radio listener to tune to CHAT-FM? A candle-lit dinner with one of the presenters? A £100 shopping spree at a supermarket? Let's take another look at the listeners that CHAT-FM's format is designed to attract. With the accent on news and views you're most likely looking at an older age group, probably 35-65, with local businesses or interests – not an easy group to bribe. But this group is settled and fairly affluent and an important target market for a number of products and services – new vehicles, for example; home improvements – and holidays, especially cruises. You have your bribe: if you're a CHAT-FM listener you're automatically entered in a draw for the Cruise of a Lifetime.

Putting it all Together

It shouldn't take a lot of imagination to apply the critical principles illustrated in those three examples into any kind of sales pitch for almost every kind of product or service. The same principles are employed whether your task is to attract 100 people to a church fête or a thousand fans to a pop concert; or to sell a used mountain bike or your farm's organic produce.

But principles, however correct, are by themselves cold concepts. Of course it is necessary to get to know what it is you're selling, to define your market, your strategy and approach, your USP and other selling points, and your clincher – the offer they can't refuse. Having done all that you have then to put your writing skills to work, to add heart and conviction and emotion, weaving all the elements into a hypnotically persuasive and irrestible pattern of words.

If you've followed the nuts and bolts of preparing to write the sales copy for the home gym, the herb window box and CHAT-FM, you couldn't do better than to sit down and as a writing exercise put it all together – whether as a sales letter, leaflet or brochure or as an advertisement.

Three young advertising copywriters were each asked to do just this, and here are their quite creditable attempts. Keep in mind that the finished work would almost certainly incorporate typography and illustration, and where appropriate, a reply coupon.

Deep down you want to be fitter, leaner, sharper, better . . .

What you want is **HOME GYM**.

Want to be fit and healthy and look your best? But don't have the time to drive to a gym? Object to paying the ever-increasing fees? Hate exercising in front of others?

Then think seriously about HOME GYM – a newly-developed muscle toning machine designed so you can exercise in the privacy of your home or flat.

40 DIFFERENT EXERCISE PROGRAMMES

HOME GYM is programmed to give you 40 different exercise regimes. Each exercise can be customised to your height and weight and stamina. A timer lets YOU be the gym instructor! It's the ultimate, scientifically personalised exercise machine for men, women and children – all the family!

UNIQUE ELECTRONIC WEIGHT CONTROL

HOME GYM is so complete it even includes a highly accurate electronic weighing platform that tells you instantly how much weight you've lost – to a gram!

A GYM IN YOUR HOME FOR JUST £249

A family subscription to the average gym is about £250 a quarter. Yet you can own this true 'gym in your home' for just that – £249 – and it's yours for life. But although it's sturdy it's amazingly light, so you can carry and use it anywhere – in your living room, the basement, the attic, the bedroom. And it dismantles quickly and easily for storage. HOME GYM is the modern miracle muscle-toning machine.

TWO FREE FITNESS VIDEOS

Every HOME GYM comes with two one-hour health and fitness videos with special exercise music tracks and full illustrated instructions.

2-WEEK FREE HOME TRIAL

We have no hesitation offering you a 2-week trial of HOME GYM. If you're not delighted just return it for a full refund. No risk!

QUALIFY NOW FOR OUR 10% DISCOUNT

Apply within 14 days and get 10% discount – it's as simple as that but it can't last. That's almost a £25 saving on your Home Gym! Don't put it off, send for your Home Gym now!

Mmm . . . I open my kitchen window – and there's a scented Mediterranean garden!

The amazing herb window box that transports the delights of a Mediterranean summer garden to your window sill.

Although herbs are surrounded by history and mystery the **Herb Garden Window Box** allows you to grow 20 different herbs easily, quickly and without any fuss.

This exotic, fragrant garden is contained in green rust-resistant trays that come in three sizes to suit any window sill. The compost is scientifically balanced to feed your garden for a whole season. All you do is water it occasionally.

A Window Box Herb Garden for just £19.99 complete
For just £19.99 and so little effort you can have a herb garden that will waft all the scents of summer into your home. You get:

Fresh herbs for **salads** – chives, parsley, lovage, tarragon
Fresh herbs for **cooking** – thyme, sage, oregano, basil, rosemary
Fresh herbs for **drinks** – mint, borage, lemon balm
Fresh herbs for **health** – chamomile, evening primrose, feverfew
Fresh herbs for **pure pleasure** – verbena, lavender, pennyroyal
Plus this FREE Edwardian-style pomander filled with traditional pillow herbs to help you sleep . . . and dream. And when your own garden ripens you can refill the pomander with your own dried, fragrant herbs! Just £19.99 buys you a beautiful, practical mini-garden from which you can pluck a variety of herbs fresh for the table. Plus the Edwardian Pomander, worth at least £10.

BUY A GARDEN FOR YOURSELF AND ONE AS A UNIQUE GIFT FOR A FRIEND – and get both herb gardens carriage free!

CHAT-FM NOW REACHES ALL YOUR FAVOURITE PLACES –
Miami, Bermuda, Bahamas, San Francisco, Hawaii
CHAT-FM is your very own radio service, bringing you local news, weather, traffic and market reports plus hourly national and international news updates on the hour.

BUT NOW CHAT-FM also reaches places you usually only dream about – Miami, Bermuda, the Bahamas . . . San Francisco, Hawaii, Tahiti . . .

BECAUSE over the next 10 weeks you could win the CHAT-FM **CRUISE OF A LIFETIME** to all those fabulous places aboard the luxury cruiseliner 'Artemia'. To enter is simple – just call the CHAT-FM Cruise Line (we broadcast the number throughout day and night) and you're automatically entered for the prize draw.

And every week you're in an additional free draw for a trip for two to Paris via Eurostar First Class. Yes, CHAT-FM is giving away **10 free luxury breaks to Paris**.

And while you're waiting for your prize you can be informed, entertained and delighted by CHAT-FM's witty team of presenters who bring you the news and views of your neighbours, besides the rich and famous.
So tune in now to **CHAT-FM 106.8**.

CHAT-FM. YOUR LOCAL STATION THAT TAKES YOU ROUND THE WORLD.

Writing in the New Millennium: Word Processing and e-mail

It came as a boon and a blessing to men,
The peaceful, the pure, the victorious PEN!

J C Prince, 1891

If letter-writing was on the wane towards the end of the 20th century (and dozens of pundits insisted that it was) then the word processor has given it new life. For the millions who despaired of their handwriting (or typing, for that matter), their lack of verbal organisation or their spelling, but who never quite lost the urge to correspond, the word processor is a gift.

With editing facility, there need be no more crossing out, no more Tippexing, no more misunderstandings, and the spell-checker can correct your howlers. So the result can look like the work of a craftsman typesetter. A click or two of your mouse, and it's printed. A couple more clicks and it's also filed – on the computers hard disk or on a small 'floppy' that can store as much as you could get into a whole old-fashioned filing cabinet. There seems little doubt that the personal computer will encourage the art and craft of writing, not depress it still further.

Another revolution is the arrival of electronic mail (e-mail) and telephone facsimile transmission (the fax). Many messages are sent by fax, to print out at the receiving end. And the use of e-mail, sent over the Internet, grows enormously every day.

You can send a fax – an A4 page should take no more 30 seconds – to most part of the world for less than the cost of first-class post. Today's e-mail users can send a fax, too, through their Internet service.

The darker side of the electronic revolution is a creeping, atrocious misuse of the English language. Putting material into the computer becomes 'inputting', a connection between two bits of hardware or software becomes an 'interface', the way a system works becomes its 'functionality'. Computer professionals are entitled to their particular jargon: anyone hoping to write decent English will have nothing to do with it.

The jargon apart, we can certainly hope for a revival in letter-writing, as more and more people realise how well the technology can help to improve your pros. The spell-check can be invaluable, as long as you remember that it will let through a wrong word if that word is in its dictionary – for example: 'He through the ball straight at the the window.' Your word-processing software may have a grammar check, too, but do not let it cramp your flowing style with some over-academic objection. Consider the suggestion that is offered and then, if you prefer your own version, ignore the checker.

No matter what the computer professional may say, no combination of technological checks and suggestions will ever create a simple sentence, in good, clear English, better than an old-fashioned human being can.

Index

WRITING GUIDES BY GRAHAM KING

Graham King's invaluable guides to good English break down the barriers that prevent so many articulate, intelligent people from communicating effectively, and increase your word power without boredom!

COLLINS IMPROVE YOUR GRAMMAR

Picking up a book on grammar takes courage, but the learner can take heart from the fact that many of the great writers, including Charlotte Bronte, were hopeless at grammar at school. This easy-to-use guide features:

- The thirteen gremlins of grammar, from apostrophes to verbs
- The point of sentence construction
- The writing of good English
- Cartoons by Hunt Emerson

COLLINS IMPROVE YOUR PUNCTUATION

Punctuation has been described as a 'courtesy designed to help readers understand a story without stumbling'. Included in this essential guide are:

- A Victorian schoolmistress's 10 Golden Rules of Punctuation
- How to deal with capitalisation, full stops and commas
- Mastery of colons, parentheses, dashes, hyphen hassle, questions, exclamations and apostrophes
- The ultimate punctuation test
- Cartoons by Hunt Emerson

COLLINS IMPROVE YOUR WRITING SKILLS

The basic principle of this incredibly useful books is that 'clarity begins at home': say what you mean and you stand a better chance of getting what you want!

- How to write clearly, and what sort of language to avoid
- How to express what you really feel in letters
- How to create the perfect CV
- Cartoons by Hunt Emerson

COLLINS COMPLETE WRITING GUIDE

A complete one-volume guide to English usage.

- Covers all aspects of writing, from grammar to foreign words and phrases, and from confusables to abbreviations.
- An authoritative and helpful guide to the writing of clear and grammatically-correct English